The Government Financial Aid Book

Student Financial Services

Published by Perpetual Press,™ Seattle, WA

Printed in the U.S.A.

Library of Congress Catalog Card Number 93-085924
ISBN 1-881199-27-4

First edition
10 9 8 7 6 5 4 3 2 1

ACKNOWLEDGMENTS

The publisher wishes to thank the following people for their contributions to *The Government Financial Aid Book*:
For the cover: Allegro Design
For the interior: Lynne Faulk Design
For composition: Jamison West
For research and editorial support: Nick Bauroth, Ali Connelly, Daisy dePaulis, Jennifer DuBois, Stefani Harris, and Ivy Tan-Torres

PUBLISHER'S NOTE

The purpose of this directory is to assist students in seeking financial aid for higher education in this country. We have designed this directory to give the readers the most accurate information possible, so they can make the best decision. We have made every effort to be as objective as possible.

Although the authors and publisher have tried to ensure the information was correct at the time of publication, phone numbers, addresses, and other financial aid information does change. This directory should only be used as a guide. Neither the authors nor the publisher assume liability for any problems the readers may encounter due to inaccurate information in this directory.

Table of Contents

Editor's Note 7

What Is Financial Aid? 8
    Loans 8
    Grants 8
    Scholarships 8
    Other Forms of Aid 8

New Laws for Higher Education Funding 9
    Student Loan Reform Act 9
    The President's Plan 9
    Community Service as a Loan Repayment Option 10

Basic Student Eligibility for Financial Aid 10

How To Use This Book 11
    High School Students 11
    Undergraduate and Graduate Students 11

Financial Aid in Review 11
    1991 to 1993 Government Aid Summary 11
    Financial Aid Process 12
    Determining Need 13
    Am I Dependent or Independent? 14

Estimating Your College Budget 15
    Private College Budget 16
    Public College Budget 16

Contribution Formulas and Worksheets 17
    Family Contribution Formula and Worksheet 17
    Student Contribution Worksheet 18
    Worksheet Instructions 19
    Budget Worksheet 21

Federal Aid Overview 22
    Grants 22
    Subsidized and Unsubsidized Loans 22

Federal Grants 23

Pell Grants 24
    How Do I Determine My Eligibility? 24
    Getting Started 24
    How Much Can I Get? 25

SEOG (Supplemental Educational Opportunity Grants) 25

How Do I Determine My Eligibility? 25

Getting Started 26

How Much Can I Get? 26

Other Forms of Aid 26

College Work-Study 26

R.O.T.C. (Reserve Officer Training Corps) 27

Federal Student Loans 29

Stafford Loans 30

How Do I Determine My Eligibility? 30

Getting Started 30

How Much Can I Get? 31

Payment 31

Payback 32

PLUS (Parental Loans for Undergraduate Students) 34

How do Parents Determine their Eligibility? 35

Getting Started 35

How Much Can I Get? 35

Payment 35

Payback 36

SLS (Supplemental Loans for Students) 37

How Do I Determine My Eligibility? 38

Getting Started 38

How Much Can I Get? 38

Payment 39

Payback 39

Deferment 40

Forbearance 40

Cancellation/Forgiveness 40

Perkins Loans 41

How Do I Determine My Eligibility? 41

Getting Started 41

How Much Can I Get? 42

Payment 42

Payback 42

Deferment 43

Forbearance 43

Cancellation/Forgiveness 43

Borrower Rights and Responsibilities 45

    How to be a Responsible Borrower 46

Loan Defaults 46

    Period Lengths 46

    Loan Consolidation 47

Emergency Loans 48

Planning for the Future 49

    Average Yearly Income for Entry Level Positions 50

    Monthly Expense Worksheet 51

State Aid Programs 53

State Aid 54

    Financial Awards by State 55

    State Agencies Listing 56

State Scholarship, Grant, and Loan Listings 62

Alternative Finance Programs 131

Alternative Ways to Pay for a College Education 132

    Tuition Prepayment Plans 132

    Guaranteed Tuition Plan 132

    Accelerated Degree Courses 132

Alternative Financing Programs 133

    Academic Management Services (AMS) 133

    Bay Banks Education Financing Programs 134

    Family Education Financing Plan (SALLIE MAE) 134

    Nellie Mae 134

    Education Resources Institute of Boston-TERI 135

    Educational Credit Corporation 135

Specialized Aid 136

High School Students 139

High School Programs 140

    Financial Aid Information Sources 140

High School Calendar 142

    Freshman Year 142

    Sophomore Year 142

    Junior Year 142

    Senior Year 143

National Phone Directory of Organizations 144

Case Study (From High School to an In-State University) 145
Sophomore Year 145
Junior Year 145
Senior Year 146

Case Study (Applying to a Private School) 146

Case Study (Applying to an Out-of-State School) 147

Forms 149

Filling Out Forms 150
Form Completion: General Rules 150

The Financial Aid Form (FAF) 152
The FAF is Used for These Programs: 152
Tips for Completing the FAF 153

The Application for Federal Student Aid (AFSA) 159
The AFSA is Used for These Programs: 159

What Happens After I Send In My Application? 165
Student Aid Report (SAR) 165
Financial Aid Application Process 167

Other Information 169

Common Financial Aid Questions 170

Financial Aid Terms and Definitions 173

Important Phone Numbers 176
Federal and State Aid Phone Numbers 176
Regional Offices 177

Reader Survey 179

Editor's Note

Attending college today is an expensive undertaking, as many people know all too well. On average, four years at a public school can cost up to $30,240, while four years at a private school can cost an average of $65,320 (tuition plus room and board). Unfortunately, most families and individual students in the United States simply cannot pay the entire bill. Help comes from both the federal government and the many private organizations which together offer over $20 billion in aid through a wide variety of programs. These government and private money sources every year give or loan money to those who need help the most. Despite the fact that money is available and waiting for rightful claimants, over $6 billion goes unclaimed every year.

To receive financial aid for college, you have to know where to look. This book is your comprehensive and complete guide to college financial aid. It informs you of application deadlines, includes valuable tips from college aid advisors, and covers topics ranging from proper completion of aid forms to applying for privately-offered scholarships. Few stones are left unturned!

As you read through this book, you will uncover almost every important source of college money available today, including state and government money offered through:

- Stafford Loans
- SLS/PLUS Loans
- Perkins Loans
- Pell Grants
- SEOG Grants
- College work-study programs
- R.O.T.C.
- State scholarships and grants

This guide helps to ensure that any student can enter college without the burden of financial stresses. The easy-to-understand material from Student Financial Services will help you avoid many of the pitfalls that students encounter during their search for college financial aid. Congratulations. You're on your way to obtaining the money you need to overcome your potentially monstrous college bills!

What Is Financial Aid?

What are some basic worries that people associate with going to college? Those that come to mind include: getting accepted at an academic institution, maintaining good grades once you're enrolled, and paying for your tuition and books for the duration of your stay. The first two worries can be put to rest by hard work and dedication to scholastic endeavors, but the third worry is a different matter altogether. Although students and their parents play an active role in the aid application process, they still have to rely on outside sources to actually give them the money they need. Who pays this money? Who's eligible to receive aid for college? What exactly is financial aid?

LOANS

Student loans are low-interest loans issued by both federal and state governments. Generally, these loans do not need to be paid back until after you graduate or leave school. Also, many loans are subsidized and do not accrue interest until you graduate. When you pay back these loans, you pay back the interest as well. The major loans we discuss in this book are:

- Stafford Loans (formerly the Guaranteed Student Loan)
- Perkins Loans
- Parental Loans for Undergraduate Students (PLUS)
- Supplemental Loans for Students (SLS)

GRANTS

Grants go to the most needy students and are most commonly issued by the federal government, state governments, and private organizations. A recipient need not excel in any academic area or activity to receive a grant. Grants are considered monetary gifts and do not need to be paid back by the recipient. The grants we discuss are:

- Pell Grants
- Supplemental Educational Opportunity Grants (SEOG)

SCHOLARSHIPS

Unlike federal grants and loans, private scholarship money is awarded on the basis of academic achievement, interest in a particular field of study, athletic ability, financial need, and a wide variety of other criteria. This type of monetary award does not need to be paid back, but some awards carry restrictions. These include requiring the student to maintain a certain g.p.a., be a member of a certain ethnic group, be active in certain student activities, be a member of a sports team, or remain in a certain field of study for the duration of one's education. Scholarship dollars come from private organizations and both state and federal aid agencies.

OTHER FORMS OF AID

If you are interested in other forms of financial aid, you can also look into aid offered by the R.O.T.C. (Reserve Officer Training Corps), College Work Study program (CWS), and various state agencies. All of these programs are discussed in this section, and a listing of every scholarship offered by each state is given.

New Laws for Higher Education Funding

STUDENT LOAN REFORM ACT

The system of student loans currently used in the U.S. has been under fire from numerous sources for its confusion and conflicts of interest. Currently, private lenders such as banks offer money to students, and the federal government backs the loans in case they cannot be repaid. There are thousands of sources of funds, so while students can apply directly to the government for grants, they must also deal with any number of forms and regulations from various institutions. In many cases, these institutions may sell the rights of the loan to another agency for collection, meaning still more paperwork. For private lenders, some of the interest on loans goes towards profits, thus increasing the cost to you. Repayment schedules are rigid, often resulting in default when borrowers have difficulty finding adequate employment after graduation. In addition, the lending institutions may not have much inclination to collect on loans at all when they know the government will pay off defaulted accounts. But legislation passed in August 1993 should change all this.

THE PRESIDENT'S PLAN

President Clinton's Student Loan Reform Act of 1993 (SLRA) won support in both the House and the Senate. Congress finally came to a resolution that will profoundly alter the way students obtain and repay their loans. The new system will save taxpayers billions of dollars.

The SLRA includes several new features. First, by the 1997-1998 academic year the federal government, through the Department of Education, will act as a direct lending agency for 60 percent of all higher education institutions. This will not only simplify the loan application process, but will also mean lower interest rates. The government is less concerned with profitability than are private institutions, so it can offer rates accordingly—perhaps even half a percentage point lower than current rates. Over the years of repayment, savings may amount to hundreds or thousands of dollars. Because the loans will be made directly, colleges can act as on-campus agents for the government, meaning that *all financial aid — grant, loan, or otherwise — can be obtained from one source.* This is, in effect, "one-stop shopping" for students in need of money for school.

Direct lending also eliminates the conflict of interest in loan collection. Because the same agency will loan and collect the money, that agency will certainly have a vested interest in ensuring the repayment of the loan. This should decrease default rates and improve the enforcement of collection. The SLRA will involve the Internal Revenue Service, which may be able to deduct payments directly from paychecks. That may sound threatening, but it is also convenient for those who don't have problems paying bills. Additionally, it will mean that the government—and taxpayers—will save money. The IRS connection is also beneficial because information on the income of borrowers will be shared with the Department of Education, and repayment schedules will be designed to reflect ability to pay. This type of repayment schedule is called income-contingent; accounts using it are known as EXCEL accounts. Flexible payments also discourage defaults and enable graduating students to accept lower-paying, community-oriented positions such as teaching or social work, without worrying about the burden of high debt. Of course, traditional payment methods of fixed-payment/fixed-term or extended-term are still options. In fact, borrowers will be able to switch plans as needed.

This year 4 percent of all post-secondary institutions will have the option of participating in a demonstration of the new federal direct loan program. Over $500 million has been set aside to fund this project. As early as 1996, all schools will be able to convert to direct lending.

COMMUNITY SERVICE AS A LOAN REPAYMENT OPTION

Another element of the SLRA concerns repayment of loans. Under President Clinton's plan, students will have the option to repay a portion of their loans through a national service program. The terms of this newly adopted program allow interested students to work for two years, either before enrollment or after graduation, in community service-oriented jobs such as teaching, law enforcement, or health care. These workers would earn a stipend, probably equivalent to minimum wage, and defray education costs at the same time. Those working before enrollment will earn financial credit, while those working during school or after graduation will have loans dismissed. The plan calls for up to 150,000 students to participate by 1997, at a cost of $3.4 billion. This year, 1,000 employees are involved in a summer demonstration project. The service program is modeled on the Civilian Conservation Corps and the GI Bill in that it provides the nation with desperately needed aid while permitting those unable to pay for an education to get one.

In 1994, over 20,000 students will be able to take part in the national service program. Following federal guidelines, state education agencies will set their own provisions for this program. Whether or not a job is considered to be "service-oriented" will be determined on an individual basis by the state. Students will be able to work a minimum of one year, part-time, to a maximum of two years, full-time. Once a student has participated in the program for two years, they are no longer eligible. The amount students earn depends on how much the federal government appropriates each year. For 1994, students may earn up to $4,700 for each year of work. Payments will be made in the form of a "voucher" which students will either take to their financial aid office or send to the agency carrying their loan. Past, present, and future borrowers are all eligible to participate in this program, making loan repayment much easier.

As of this writing, the specific provisions of the newly passed Student Loan Reform Act have not been set. The demonstration project will serve as a basis for further guidelines in both the federal direct loan and the national service programs. Look for upcoming information at your school's financial aid office.

Basic Student Eligibility for Financial Aid

Post-secondary education is a huge investment, but receiving aid—whether it comes in the form of grants, loans, or scholarships—can relieve a large portion of that financial stress. Anyone who needs help should apply for financial aid to cover college costs. *Before you apply for federal, state, or even private aid, make sure that you meet the following criteria:*

• Have a high school diploma or a General Education Development (GED)

• Be a U.S. citizen, a U.S. national status, or a permanent resident

• Have a social security number (exceptions for non-citizens)

• Be a half or full-time student who is enrolled, or will be enrolling, in an accredited college or university

- Be registered with the Selective Service (male applicants only)
- Have not defaulted on any previously received federal financial aid

If you have any questions concerning these eligibility requirements, check with a financial aid counselor or call the Federal Student Aid Information Center at (800) 4FED-AID.

How To Use This Book

The way in which each student uses the information provided in this book depends mainly on your individual needs and year in school. It's important to note that high school, undergraduate, and graduate students all have very different levels of financial aid need. Students should take these factors into consideration before they start applying.

The following list suggests a few ways students can use the information given in this book:

HIGH SCHOOL STUDENTS

- Become familiar with all types of financial aid available
- Learn how to receive aid from all sources (federal, state, and private)
- Estimate the entire cost of an undergraduate education
- Determine the amount of money you need to contribute to your education
- Construct and follow a detailed financial aid plan
- Increase your eligibility for aid from private, state, and federal scholarships and grants

UNDERGRADUATE AND GRADUATE STUDENTS

- Stay current on new financial aid rules and regulations
- Determine how much aid you are eligible for from loans, grants, and scholarships
- Plan ahead for loan repayments after college graduation
- Find out about loan deferment and cancellation
- Apply for state-funded undergraduate and graduate scholarships

Financial Aid in Review

1991 TO 1993 GOVERNMENT AID SUMMARY

Despite rising college costs and an increase in the number of students applying for aid, the government continues to provide assistance to more students every year. The following chart shows increases in the yearly number of students receiving aid and illustrates how the government awards money to almost everyone who needs it. Since 1991, nearly every federal aid program has increased the supply of money to a growing number of needy students.

Number of Students Receiving Aid

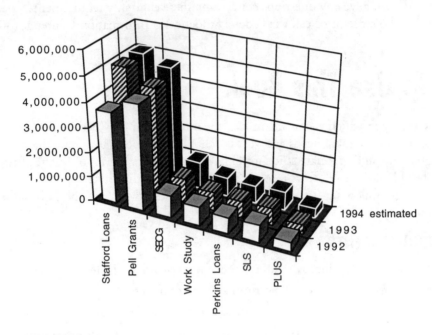

FINANCIAL AID PROCESS

20 Simple Steps to Financial Aid Success

1. Choose a college or university
2. Contact the school's financial aid office for:
    - -total college costs
    - -financial aid information
    - -financial aid procedures, applications, and deadlines
3. Graduate from high school or take the GED
4. Correctly fill out the required financial aid forms and make copies of all completed forms
5. Send the forms in as far ahead of the deadline as you can
6. Receive the Student Aid Report (SAR), review the form, and make any corrections
7. Send the SAR to the financial aid office at your school. Keep a copy for your own records
8. Receive and review the award letter telling you what aid you are eligible to receive
9. Accept all or part of the aid package
10. Sign and return the award letter to the financial aid office
11. Apply for a loan:
    - -Stafford
    - -SLS
    - -PLUS

12.   Choose a lender

13.   Get a loan application from the financial aid office, fill it out, and send it to your lender

14.   Receive loan approval

15.   Start school

16.   Maintain good grades and aid eligibility

17.   Complete a financial aid application *every year*

18.   Follow the same steps each year

19.   Keep track of your loans

20.   Graduate from college!

DETERMINING NEED

"Need" is a very important criterion used by the government to determine an applicant's total award. Because of the rising costs of attending a college or university, the number of current and prospective college students who need financial assistance has risen dramatically. What constitutes "need?" In order to show need, you do not have to be living below poverty level. The government decides that you need money for college when your family, or you alone, cannot finance your whole education. Theoretically, those who need the most money will receive the highest reward.

To help you determine an estimate of your need, we have provided you with a simple equation and some helpful definitions.

The Need Formula

Total Cost of College - Family Contribution = Financial Need

The exact calculation of financial need is performed by private companies (such as, College Scholarship Services or American College Testing) who calculate these figures for colleges, private institutions, and government agencies. The preceding formula is used when evaluating need for Stafford Loan programs. A different formula is used for the Pell Grant program to determine your Pell Grant Index number.

Total Cost of College

> Tuition
> + Books and supplies
> + Housing costs
> + Meals
> + Personal expenses
> + Transportation
> + Support of dependents
> + Any other miscellaneous expenses
> = TOTAL COST OF COLLEGE

QUICK TIP: *If you do not know exact costs for a specific school because you have yet to attend, then request an estimate from the school's financial aid office (they often have them readily available). Because most schools require that you submit your aid application by January 1st of the year in which you need aid, you should begin figuring out your "need" the previous fall.*

13

Family Contribution

The federal government believes that it is the family's responsibility to put it's children through college. However, if your parents can't meet all of the rising costs of higher education, financial aid is available. The family contribution is a dollar amount that you and your family pay toward the cost of college for the coming year. To determine your family contribution (FC), a formula, called the Congressional Methodology is employed. Congressional Methodology, developed by Congress under the Higher Education Amendment of 1986, evaluates parents' income and assets, then compares it to the number of children who are college-aged in the family and the expected incurred costs of higher education. However, everything your parents own is not included in this calculation. The government realizes the amount of assets a family may have is not necessarily a good indication of whether or not they can afford to put their children through school. To protect your parents' savings, when the family contribution is calculated, home, farm and a percentage of the overall assets are not included. From this evaluation, the family contribution figure and the child's need eligibility is determined for campus-based, state, and federal aid programs.

Student Contribution

Parents are not the only ones who are expected to partially finance a college education. The federal government also presumes that a substantial portion of your income and savings will go towards your college expenses. On average, at least half of your prospective income, and 35 percent of your savings (if you have any), will be included in your expected contribution. But don't worry, you won't be paying the same amount throughout college. The amount of your contribution changes every year in correlation to your income. If you make less money your first year in school, you'll be eligible for more aid the following year.

Once the total family contribution has been calculated through the need analysis procedure, the final numbers are sent to the colleges or universities of your choice. The financial aid office at each institution analyzes your financial situation in comparison to the total cost of your education. The school then determines if you are eligible to receive aid, and if so, how much. Each college financial aid office has its own set of criteria for evaluating need, and adjustments are made after an initial number has been determined by either CSS or ACT.

If you would like to know more about the congressional methodology formula, write to either of the following addresses for a free booklet on the formula:

Formula Book
Department DED-87
Pueblo, CO 81009

Federal Student Aid Information Center
P.O. Box 84
Washington, DC 20044

QUICK TIP: Home and farm equity are no longer included in the government's determination of total assets for all families. The government also figures in an assets protection benefit, a percentage of your parents' assets that are not included in the total figure.

To get an idea of what you and your parents will be contributing to your education, complete the sample exercises on the following pages. This is the formula companies like ACT and CSS use to determine the family contribution figure.

AM I DEPENDENT OR INDEPENDENT?

One common factor involved in all federal and state aid applications is determining your status as dependent or independent from your parents. Students who are claimed on their parents' yearly income tax forms and who receive financial support from their parents are classified as *dependents*. When filing for financial aid, dependent students must report their parents' yearly income and assets on their aid applications. *Independent* students are financially self-supporting and are not claimed by their parents for tax purposes. It's important for you to know how the government determines your status.

Students qualify as independents if they:

- Are at least 24 years old by December 31 of the award year
- Are a U.S. Armed Forces veteran
- Are an orphan or ward of the court
- Have legal dependents other than a spouse (that is, have children), and pay at least half of their support
- Are married and are no longer claimed on parents' income tax returns
- Have not been claimed as a dependent on parents' income taxes for the past two calendar years. For this to be true, students:

  -Must earn more than $4,000 per year from income and benefits

  -Cannot live with parents for six or more consecutive weeks during the year

  -Must not have received $750 or more from parents within the year

The U.S. government believes a child's parents are chiefly responsible for their childrens' education whether or not they are classified as independent. Until recently, dependent students were able to claim themselves as independents in order to receive more financial aid from federal and state governments. Now, however, strict guidelines prohibit this practice. Under new laws, the parents of independent students may still have to provide income and asset information on financial aid applications.

If you answer "no" to all of the following questions, your parents must submit financial information whether you are classified as an independent or a dependent.

1. Were you born *before* January 1, 1970?	Yes_____	No_____
2. Are you a graduate or professional student?	Yes_____	No_____
3. Are you a veteran of the armed forces?	Yes_____	No_____
4. Are you married?	Yes_____	No_____
5. Are both your parents deceased or are you a ward of the Court?	Yes_____	No_____
6. Do you have legal dependents other than a spouse?	Yes_____	No_____

If you answer "yes" to any of these questions and are independent, then your parents do not need to provide financial information on your application forms.

For more information on this subject, contact your financial aid office, or call (800) 4FED-AID.

Estimating Your College Budget

Apply for financial aid before deciding which college or university you are going to attend. High school seniors are not usually notified of acceptance at an institution until long after the deadline to apply for aid has come and gone. For many students, the amount of aid they will be eligible to receive determines the school they choose to attend. It's very important to estimate the general costs of each institution you are considering.

College costs differ greatly from one campus to another and depend on several factors. Whether or not you live on campus, attend an in-state or out-of-state school, or work during the year all influence the amount of money you will need to cover expenses. When estimating your school budget, include the basic costs of tuition, room and board, and books and supplies, but don't forget money for yourself. One of the most common mistakes students make in budgeting is not to consider money for personal expenses such as clothing, transportation, medical bills, and recreation.

The following five budgets are from different colleges over one academic period. Using these examples, complete the worksheets on the following pages with your own projected budget for the six colleges of your choice.

QUICK TIP: *Don't be discouraged if some of your estimates are high. Expensive colleges usually have more financial aid available to help their students meet the higher costs involved.*

PRIVATE COLLEGE BUDGET

	Student Commutes	Student Lives on Campus
Tuition	$12,000	$12,000
Room & Board	$1,720	$4,550
Books & Supplies	$488	$488
Transportation	$750	$468
Personal Expenses	$1,200	$1,450
TOTAL COST:	$16,158	$18,956

PUBLIC COLLEGE BUDGET

	Student Commutes	Student Lives on Campus	Out-of-State Student
Tuition	$2,100	$2,100	$6,300
Room & Board	$1,569	$3,561	$3,561
Books & Supplies	$477	$477	$477
Transportation	$750	$468	$810
Personal Expenses	$1,200	$1,450	$1,600
TOTAL COST:	$6,096	$8,056	$12,748

Contribution Formulas and Worksheets

FAMILY CONTRIBUTION FORMULA AND WORKSHEET

A. INCOME & TAXES	Joe Smith's	Yours
Parent's Total Income:	$33,400	$_____
U.S. Income Tax Paid:	- 2,543	-_____
Social Security Tax Paid:	- 2,555	-_____
State and Other Taxes:	- 2,672	-_____
Employment Allowance:	- 2,500	-_____
Income Protection Allowance:	- 17,290	-_____
Available Income:	= 5,840	=_____

B. REAL ESTATE & ASSETS	Joe Smith's	Yours
Net Worth of Real Estate and Investments:	$3,000	$_____
Business & Farm (net worth):	+ 0	+_____
Cash, Checking, & Savings:	+ 3,000	+_____
Net Worth:	= 6,000	=_____
Education Savings/Asset Protection:	-44,300	-_____
Discretionary Net Worth:	= -38,300	=_____
Asset Conversion Rate:	x 12%	x 12%
Income Supplement:	= 0	=_____

C. CONTRIBUTION	Joe Smith's	Yours
Available Income:	$5,840	$_____
Income Supplement (negative, use 0):	+ 0	+_____
Adjusted Available Income:	= 5,840	=_____
AAI Taxation Rate:	x 22%	x_____
Total Contribution:	= 1,285	=_____
Multiple Children in College:	*Divide by # of students (ex. 2)*	_____
Parents' Contribution:	= 643	=_____

The American College Testing Program granted permission for the reproduction of the following calculations and figures from the 1993-94 edition of "Applying for Financial Aid."
This information has not been reviewed or approved by the U.S. Department of Education.

STUDENT CONTRIBUTION WORKSHEET

A. INCOME & TAXES	Joe Smith's	Yours
Student's Total Income:	- $3,520	$ _____
U.S. Income Tax Paid:	- 0	- _____
Social Security Tax Paid:	- 269	- _____
State & Local Income Tax:	- 141	- _____
Income Protection Allowance:	- 1,750	- 1,750
Available Income:	= 1,360	= _____
Assessment Rate:	x .5	x .5
Available Income:	= 680	= _____

B. REAL ESTATE & ASSETS	Joe Smith's	Yours
Cash, Savings, & Checking:	$765	$ _____
Real estate & Investments (net):	+ 0	+ _____
Business/Farm (net worth):	+ 0	+ _____
Discretionary Net Worth:	= 765	= _____
Asset Conversion Rate:	x .35	x .35
Income Supplement:	= 268	= _____
Contribution From Available Income:	+ 680	+ _____
Student's Contribution:	= 948	= _____

Once both figures have been calculated, the parents' and student's expected contribution is added together to determine the total family contribution.

Student's Contribution:	$ 948	$ _____
Parents' Contribution:	+ 643	+ _____
Total Family Contribution:	= 1,591	= _____

A student's eligibility for financial aid is then determined by subtracting the expected educational costs from the *total family contribution:*

Educational Costs:	$8,500	$ _____
Total Family Contribution:	- 1,591	- _____
Assistance Needed:	= 6,909	= _____

WORKSHEET INSTRUCTIONS

A. SOCIAL SECURITY TAX

Earnings between:	**Taxes will be**:
$0-55,500	7.65% of total income
$55,501-130,200	$4,245.75 + 1.45% of earnings over $55,500 (maximum of $5,328)

State and Other Taxes (averages)

Earnings between:	**Taxes will be:**
$0-$14,999	9% of total income
$15,000 or more	

Employment Allowance

# of Working Parents:	**Allowance:**
1	35% of the smaller of the two employment incomes or $2,500 (the lesser amount)
2	Also 35% or $2,500 (the lesser amount)

Income Protection Allowance

# of Family Members (+ student):	**# of Students in College (for additional students - $1,790):**
	One student
2	$10,520
3	13,100
4	16,180
5	19,090
6	22,330

for each additional member + $2,520

B. ADJUSTED NET WORTH OF BUSINESS/FARM

Market value of business/farm	$_____
Debt	-_____
Total net worth	=_____

2. **Total net worth**	**Adjusted net worth:**
< $1	$0
$1-$75,000	40% of net worth
$75,001-$225,000	$30,000 + 50% of excess over $75,000
$225,001-$375,000	$105,000 + 60% of excess over $225,000
$375,001 or more	$195,000 + 100% of excess over $375,000

Education Savings and Asset Protection Allowance

Age of Older Parent	2 Parent	1 Parent
35-39	$25,900	$19,000
40-44	34,100	24,700
45-49	38,800	27,600
50-54	44,300	31,100
55-59	51,300	35,200
60-64	60,300	40,300
65+	66,800	44,000

asset conversion rate: 12%

C. ADJUSTED AVAILABLE INCOME TAXATION

If AAI is:	Parental Contribution is:
$-3,410 or less	$-750
-3,409 - 9,400	AAI x 22%
9,401 - 11,800	[(AAI -9,400) x 25%] = 2,068
11,801 - 14,200	[(AAI - 14,200) x 34%] = 2,668
14,201 - 16,600	[(AAI - 16,600) x 40%] = 3,364
16,601 - 19,000	[(AAI - 19,000) x 47%] = 5,140

D. SOCIAL SECURITY TAX

Total income:	Tax:
$0-$55,500	7.65 % of total income
$55,501 - $130,200	$4,245.75 + 1.45% of excess over $55,500 (maximum of $5,328)

Since tax allowances vary by state, use 4% of your total income.

BUDGET WORKSHEET

	College A	_College B_
Tuition	_____	_____
Room & Board	_____	_____
Books & Supplies	_____	_____
Transportation	_____	_____
Personal Expenses	_____	_____
TOTAL COST:	$	$

	College C	_College D_
Tuition	_____	_____
Room & Board	_____	_____
Books & Supplies	_____	_____
Transportation	_____	_____
Personal Expenses	_____	_____
TOTAL COST:	$	$

	College E	_College F_
Tuition	_____	_____
Room & Board	_____	_____
Books & Supplies	_____	_____
Transportation	_____	_____
Personal Expenses	_____	_____
TOTAL COST:	$	$

Federal Aid Overview

Without a doubt, federal and state government agencies provide more money to students for school than any other organization or agency. In 1993, federal government education programs will insure almost $27 billion dollars in student aid, handed out in the form of secured loans, grants, and scholarships (see graph on page 12).

Throughout this section we refer to the SAR, an acronym for Student Aid Report. After an applicant's request for Federal Aid dollars is processed, they receive an SAR, telling them: 1) whether they may receive a Pell Grant, 2) their Pell Grant Index number, 3) their family contribution number, and 4) if they have failed to fill the form out correctly. The financial aid advisor at your college uses this report to help organize your aid package. Call (301) 722-9200 to receive an extra copy of your SAR.

This portion of the book details the major loans and grants offered by the government, and how to apply for and receive aid dollars for which you are eligible. In order to help you understand how each program works, we divided this section according to related government programs as well as dollar availability.

GRANTS

Rejoice if you receive all of your financial aid from federal grants. Grants constitute "free money" for students. These dollars are free because they accrue no interest and do not need to be repaid. Every year, both the Pell Grant and SEOG programs provide these funds to thousands of college students nationwide.

SUBSIDIZED AND UNSUBSIDIZED LOANS

Students and their parents should be aware that government loans may be either fully subsidized or unsubsidized. A subsidized loan does not accrue interest until the student graduates or leaves school. Unsubsidized loans are less desirable because interest on the total loan amount accrues while the student is in school. Here is a breakdown of government subsidized and/or unsubsidized loans:

- Stafford Loan: These loans are either subsidized or unsubsidized. Your school makes the final determination based on financial need.
- PLUS: These loans are unsubsidized, accruing interest while the student is in school.
- SLS: These loans are unsubsidized, accruing interest while the student is in school.
- Perkins Loan: These loans are subsidized by the government.

Federal Grants

Student Financial Services

Pell Grants

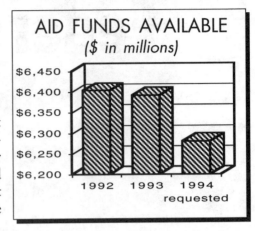

AID FUNDS AVAILABLE
($ in millions)

- No payback is necessary
- Source: Federal government
- Deadlines: Application must be received no later than the first week of May (find out the exact date from your advisor). Your Student Aid Report (SAR) is due to your school's financial aid advisor near the end of June or the last day of school enrollment (deadlines for 1994-1995 school year are May 2 and June 30 of 1994)

The federal government's Pell Grant program deserves its good reputation. In 1993, nearly $6.4 billion was awarded to the neediest students (see figure at right). Every eligible student will receive a Pell Grant (the size of which depends on the individual student). This program is specifically designed to help undergraduate students finance their education for up to six years of study without burdening them with a repayment plan. Nothing needs to be repaid to the government and there is no interest or loan fee.

HOW DO I DETERMINE MY ELIGIBILITY?

- Your Pell Grant Index (PGI) number must be low enough to meet required need standards, as determined by the government
- You must be attending school no less than half-time
- You must be working on your first undergraduate degree
- You must meet all application deadlines
- You must be a U.S. citizen or permanent resident

QUICK TIP: Do you want to know how your PGI number is calculated? A lengthy formula is used, but you can see how it works by writing to the following address for a free formula book:

Federal Student Aid Information Center
P.O. Box 84
Washington, DC 20044

GETTING STARTED

If you know that you will be needing some sort of federal or state financial aid, you should apply for this grant first. To apply for a Pell Grant, you must obtain and complete either the Financial Aid Form or Application for Federal Student Aid. Samples of these forms can be found beginning on page 155. To obtain the form, contact your school's financial aid office or call your state's guarantee agency (see state agency listings on page 56). Be sure to send your Pell Grant application to the address on the form as soon after January 1 as possible, because missing the deadlines means missing out on financial aid. Call (800) 4FED-AID for answers to any questions you might have. Applicants can find out the status of their application by calling (301) 722-9200. This office will not accept collect calls. If all goes according to plan, you will receive your three-part SAR within six weeks. If you have failed to fill out the form correctly, you will have to resubmit Part 2, the Information Request Form, before your eligibility can be determined.

HOW MUCH CAN I GET?

Before any Pell Grant money can be awarded, the three-part SAR must be submitted to the school's financial aid office. Once again, students who do not meet established deadlines will receive nothing. The official application deadline is usually the last day of your institution's regular school year, or around the end of June. In 1993, Pell Grant recipients are eligible to receive up to $2,300. All award money is distributed by the schools as either a credit to the student's account or a direct distribution. Total award amounts depend on your PGI number, cost of education, and a variety of other factors. Contact a financial aid advisor at your school immediately to find out exactly what is required.

QUICK TIP: *If you choose to fill out the FAF for financial aid, you may check "Yes" in the box that authorizes the release of information in Section B. If you do this, your PGI number will be determined automatically .*

SEOG (Supplemental Educational Opportunity Grants)

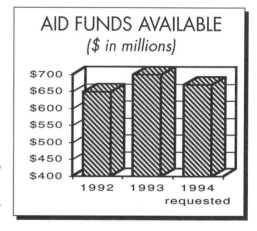

- No payback is necessary
- Campus-based program
- Source: Government provides money to schools for grants
- Deadlines: Usually around January 1; actual deadline is set by the school

SEOG is an acronym for Supplemental Educational Opportunity Grants. In 1993, this campus-based government grant program provided nearly $700 million to financially needy students (see figure at right). Funding for SEOG comes from the government, but administration of grants is done by the school. Most often, those who receive a Pell Grant will be given priority for a SEOG.

HOW DO I DETERMINE MY ELIGIBILITY?

- You must be attending a school that awards SEOGs
- You must show a high degree of financial need, as determined by the school
- Most recipients are full-time students, but those attending school half-time or less may also receive a grant
- You must be working on first undergraduate or graduate degree

QUICK TIP: *Apply early because at most schools this money is quickly disbursed.*

GETTING STARTED

No trick here: once you're enrolled in school, talk to your financial aid advisor. He or she will tell you how to apply, what form to complete, and answer any questions you may have. Ask when the financial aid office will begin accepting SEOG applications and what criteria are used by the school to determine financial need. After completing the paperwork, return it to the financial aid office and try to determine how long it will take before you hear about your award.

HOW MUCH CAN I GET?

The recipient of this grant can hope to receive up to $4,000 a year, depending on financial need. Generally, your school will pay you or credit your account at least once per quarter or semester. Apply early or you may miss out.

Other Forms of Aid

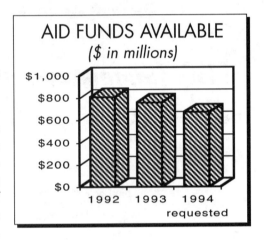

Federal and state-funded grants and loans for school are the two most important sources of financial aid for students with need. However, two other federal programs exist that also provide much needed aid to students. Both the College Work-Study Program (CWS) and the U.S. Armed Forces R.O.T.C. program make financial aid dollars available to those who meet their qualifications. CWS may become part of any student's total financial aid package and the amount is determined by a school's financial aid advisor. R.O.T.C. gives scholarships to students who apply to the program and agree to meet various eligibility criteria. Program details for both the CWS and R.O.T.C. are given here.

COLLEGE WORK-STUDY

- Campus-based program
- Source: Federal government pays 80 percent of wages; employer pays the remaining 20 percent
- Deadlines: Schools determine their own deadlines (usually shortly after January 1)

The College Work-Study Program (CWS) is another campus-based financial aid program, but it is vastly different from both the Perkins Loan and SEOG Grant programs. This particular program provides over $800 million to undergraduate and graduate students, enabling them to round out their total financial aid package by working for the remainder of their allowable aid money (see figure above). Schools will allow this sort of financial aid for those who have shown adequate financial need. CWS participants not only receive money for their education, but also get on-the-job experience that is beneficial down the road. Most jobs must relate to the student's field of study and can be found on campus or with non-profit organizations.

How Do I Determine My Eligibility?

- You must be working on first undergraduate or graduate degree
- You must show adequate financial need, as determined by the school
- You can attend school full-time, half-time, or less than half-time
- You must apply before application deadlines have passed
- You must find a suitable work-study job if the school has not provided one for you

Getting Started

When students visit their financial aid office, they should be ready to ask about CWS program details. Students may either apply specifically for CWS or it may automatically become part of their financial aid. The actual application process may vary somewhat from school to school, so each student is advised to check with their financial aid advisor for details. Deadlines? Every school sets its own, and you must meet them, because campus-based aid dollars are used up quickly.

How Much Can I Get?

Hourly pay ultimately depends on the job requirements and worker's qualifications. However, whether on or off campus, every job will pay at least the federal minimum wage. The number of allowable work-study hours any student may accumulate is closely regulated by the financial aid office in an effort to avoid situations whereby the individual earns more than their established need. Your financial aid advisor can tell you how work schedules are set and what circumstances must exist in order for you to participate in the program.

R.O.T.C. (RESERVE OFFICER TRAINING CORPS)

Armed Forces R.O.T.C.

- No monetary payback is required
- Source: U.S. Armed Forces
- Deadlines: High school students should talk to a recruiter or a guidance counselor during early spring of their junior year; college students can contact the R.O.T.C. office on their campus

R.O.T.C. is an acronym for Reserve Officer Training Corps, the military's college-based program for officer training. This program can offer both college financial aid assistance and a post-college career in the Army, Navy, Marines, or Air Force. The military provides an opportunity for specialized training that may not otherwise be available in a regular course of study. The R.O.T.C. can be a very rewarding experience for the right person.

How Do I Determine My Eligibility?

- You must be actively enrolled in a participating school
- You must pass stringent physical examinations
- You must achieve satisfactory scores on the college entrance examinations (for example SAT or ACT) required by the school

- You must commit to active and inactive duty as required by the military after completion of school
- You must meet specific military selection criteria (such as character evaluation, passing military written exam, etc.)
- You must meet other miscellaneous requirements set by each branch of the military

Getting Started

Potential applicants should speak to their guidance counselor or a local military recruiter about this program. Generally, college students must have at least two years of study remaining and should visit the R.O.T.C. building on or near campus to find out details. Interested applicants can obtain a myriad of useful information by writing or calling the following sources (also see page 176):

Army R.O.T.C.
Headquarters Cadet Command
Fort Monroe, VA 23651
(800) USA-ROTC

Air Force R.O.T.C.
College Scholarship Branch
Maxwell Air Force Base
Maxwell, AL 36117-6663
(800) 423-USAF

Navy-Marine Corps R.O.T.C. Program
Recruiting Command
801 North Randolf Street
Arlington, VA 22203-1992
(800) NAV-ROTC

How Much Can I Get?

Students in an R.O.T.C. Program can expect to receive either a two- or four-year tuition scholarship; non-scholarship programs exist, too. Scholarships pay for your R.O.T.C. books and lab fees as well as some or all of your other college expenses. A monthly nontaxable stipend of around $100 is commonplace, and helps cover some of your personal expenses. Depending on the size of the scholarship, post-college military commitment is usually four years active duty and four years reserve duty (time commitments vary). In all cases, R.O.T.C. students must complete military coursework in addition to their regular academic coursework. You can thoroughly investigate this college financial aid option by contacting the preceding list of sources.

Federal Student Loans

Student Financial Services

Stafford Loans

- Stafford Loans must be repaid
- Lender: Banks, credit unions, savings and loans, loan associations, schools
- Insurance: Insured by lender and re-insured by the state and/or federal government
- Interest rates: Variable. Three-month Treasury Bill rate plus 3.1% adjusted annually (with a 9% cap) for borrowers after October 1, 1992. Most loans are subsidized and interest-free until graduation
- Deadlines: Apply as soon after January 1st as possible

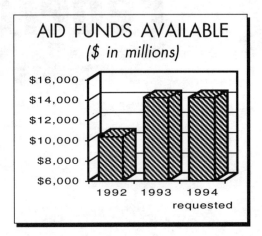

The Stafford Loan was formerly known as the Guaranteed Student Loan or GSL and currently provides more aid dollars than any other individual government educational aid program. In 1993, approximately $14 billion was given out (see graph above). Stafford Loans are issued by many different lending institutions and are fully insured by both the state and federal governments.

HOW DO I DETERMINE MY ELIGIBILITY?

- You must be enrolled at least half-time in a participating school
- You must be a U.S. citizen, national, or registered alien
- Stafford Loans are now issued to any student regardless of income. Students are able to borrow money whether in financial need or not
- Students studying overseas are also eligible as long as they are earning credit from their state institution
- You must not have previously defaulted on any other student aid loans
- Junior and senior undergraduates must not have more than $23,000 outstanding from previous Stafford Loans (or GSLs), and graduate students must not have more than $65,000 outstanding from any previous Staffords or GSLs

GETTING STARTED

To receive a Stafford Loan, you must first choose a lender in your state (do this after you're accepted into your school). You should first contact your state's guarantee agency. We have compiled a full state-by-state list of these agencies for you (see page 56) or you can call (800) 4FED-AID. Your state's agency will tell you about lender options.

QUICK TIP: *Before taking the time to seek out a lender, go to your family's bank to see if they issue Stafford Loans. If they don't, they can probably recommend a bank that does.*

All applicants need to fill out the FAF or AFSA (see page 150) and submit this to the school in which they are currently enrolled or plan to attend. After your financial aid package is complete, including the amount you are eligible to borrow, you will either receive a Stafford Loan application in the mail from your financial aid office or you'll need to request one. Complete the form carefully and take it directly to your chosen lender or back to the financial aid office. They will transfer it for you. Make sure that the school you're attending has filled out its section of the form, certifying your registration, the amount of financial aid you will be receiving, and the total cost of your tuition and expenses. (CSS or ACT determines need.) Before you can receive a Stafford Loan, your school will automatically check your eligibility for a Pell Grant before announcing the appropriate loan amount. If you do receive a Pell Grant, the amount of your Stafford Loan may be less. In some cases, your college or university can certify a loan for less money than you're eligible to receive, or they can refuse to certify your application altogether. If this does happen, the school must present you with written documentation for its actions. The school's decision is final and cannot be appealed to the U.S. Department of Education.

HOW MUCH CAN I GET?

The following figures represent the maximum amount of money that anyone can receive annually through the Stafford Loan program:

- First year undergraduate students: $2,625
- Second year undergraduate students: $3,500
- Third and fourth year undergraduate students and beyond: $5,500
- Graduate students enrolled on or after October 1, 1993: $8,500

Undergraduate students who won't be attending school for a full academic year are still eligible for a Stafford Loan. The amount all students receive cannot exceed the total cost of their education minus the amount of other financial aid awarded:

```
  Cost of education
- Other financial aid
= STAFFORD LOAN AMOUNT
```

Your total outstanding Stafford Loan balance depends on your year in school. Undergraduates may have no more than $23,000 in loan debt. The maximum amount for graduate and professional students is $65,000. This figure also includes any money borrowed during undergraduate study. These amounts apply only to loans received on or after July 1, 1993. If you do not fall in this category, contact your financial aid office for the correct figures.

PAYMENT

Once the application for your Stafford Loan has been approved by the lender, the funds will automatically be transferred back to your school for disbursement. Before receiving your loan payment, you must sign a promissory note agreeing to pay back the entire amount you have borrowed. The disbursement of loans is either credited to your account by the school or paid directly to you (or both). The number of payments you receive is based on your academic calendar. If you attend a school on the quarter system, you'll usually be paid three times a year at the start of each quarter. Schools that operate on a semester system pay their students twice a year, at the beginning of fall and spring terms. With the Stafford Loan, disbursements may also be on an equal weekly or monthly installment plan. Payments may never be more than one-half the amount of your loan. Students who are studying overseas can arrange to receive their funds directly.

Undergraduate students in their first year of study who are also first-time Stafford Loan borrowers must wait thirty days after the start of school to receive their first loan installment. This also applies to borrowers attending an institution with a default rate over thirty percent. Contact your financial aid office for more information. Because of this waiting period, it is very important that you make arrangements to have your tuition and expenses covered until you receive your installment. Many schools will grant emergency loans free of interest to students who have not yet received financial aid (see page 48 for more emergency loan information).

PAYBACK

Interest

The interest rate on the Stafford Loan varies. Students who received their first federally funded loan on or after October 1, 1992, have a variable interest rate set every year in June. On June 30, 1993, the interest rate was set at 6.22%. The rates cannot exceed 9% and you will be notified by the organization carrying your loan after they have been changed. If you have a Stafford Loan but do not fit in the category described above, contact your lender for the current interest rate.

Students who have Stafford Loans based on need are not responsible for making interest payments until after graduation. These types of loans are "subsidized," meaning that the Federal government supports or pays the interest on these loans while the borrower is in school. In accordance with the 1993-94 financial aid revisions, "non-need" or "unsubsidized" loans will accrue interest while the student is in school and during deferment periods. Borrowers with unsubsidized loans may have the option of letting interest accumulate until they are out of school or until deferment ends.

In addition to the interest you pay and the principal itself, students with subsidized loans will be charged a 5% "origination fee" that is deducted equally from each payment. The origination fee helps the federal government cover the costs for the Stafford Loan program. Some lending institutions may also collect an insurance premium of up to 3%. This premium is deducted from installments in the same way as the origination fee. Students with unsubsidized loans will be charged a combined origination fee and insurance premium of 6.5%, deducted from each payment.

Installments

Your payback plan goes into effect six months after you graduate, leave school, or reduce your enrollment to less than half-time. If you have a subsidized Stafford Loan, you are not responsible for interest payments during this six-month period. If your loan is unsubsidized, interest will continue to accumulate.

If your status changes, you must notify the organization carrying your loan. Often this organization will be different from the original lender, because many sell the loans they carry to other companies who handle the collection process.

QUICK TIP: *By law, you must be notified if the original lender sells your loan to another organization. Both companies should notify you of the sale and provide you with information about the new organization carrying your loan.*

Within four months of the grace period, the organization carrying your loan should inform you of the date repayment is to begin. However, if this deadline has passed and the company has not contacted you, it is your responsibility to either notify the organization or begin repayment on time.

Stafford payments are typically made over a five- to ten-year period, depending on the size of your loan; the minimum monthly payment is $50.

QUICK TIP: *If your loan was first disbursed on or after July 1, 1993, you have a new repayment option. You can repay your loan on an "income-contingency" basis, meaning your financial income will determine the amount of your monthly payments.*

This chart gives an example of a typical repayment period for Stafford Loans with an interest rate of 9%. The highest rate possible is 9%, so it's likely your rates will be much lower.

Loan Amount	# of Payments	Monthly	Total Repaid
$2,600	66	$50.00	$3,307.65
$4,000	120	$50.67	$6,080.44
$7,500	120	$95.01	$11,400.82
$10,000	120	$126.68	$15,201.09
$15,000	120	$190.01	$22,801.64

Deferment

Deferring or postponing Stafford Loan payments is possible under specific conditions as long as the loan is not in default. You must contact the agency carrying your loan to apply for deferment. Be prepared to present documentation to support your request. Your eligibility for deferment depends on the date your loan was first disbursed, the current status of your loan, and the following:

LOANS FIRST DISBURSED ON OR AFTER JULY 1, 1993

Deferment is granted for:

- Graduate or fellowship study
- Half- or full-time enrollment in a post-secondary institution
- Involvement in rehabilitation programs for the physically challenged

Up to three years deferment is granted for:

- Economic difficulties
- Inability to find full-time employment

If your Stafford Loan was not disbursed on or after July 1, 1993, contact the organization holding your loan for deferment guidelines

QUICK TIP: *If you have a subsidized Stafford Loan, you must still make interest payments during the deferment period.*

Forbearance

Any student who is willing to make loan payments but is unable to do so, and who is not eligible for a deferment, may apply for "forbearance." Forbearance is a specified amount of time during which you are not required to make any payments on the principal balance or interest of your loan. You must contact the organization that carries your loan and inquire about procedures to apply for forbearance. Most companies require some type of written statement about your present financial situation.

Cancellation/Forgiveness

The repayment of a Stafford Loan may be cancelled or forgiven, but only under the following specific conditions.

Up to 100% forgiveness:

- Bankruptcy (in some cases)
- Complete and permanent disability of the borrower (100%)
- Death of the borrower (100%)
- Going back to school for a teaching certificate
- Teaching full-time in an area serving low-income students
- Teaching full-time in an area with a shortage of teachers
- Working full-time as a nurse
- Volunteering for the Peace Corps, VISTA, or other nonprofit organization

QUICK TIP: *The Department of Defense may repay a portion of your Stafford Loan as an incentive for you to enlist. Contact a local recruiting officer for more information.*

If you qualify for any one of these requirements and would like to apply for cancellation, contact the organization carrying your loan. Some of these conditions are dependent on the amount of funds available to cover such programs, so check with your loan company for availability.

Remember, any questions or concerns about Stafford repayment, cancellation, deferment, or borrower responsibilities must be directed to the organization carrying your loan.

PLUS (Parental Loans for Undergraduate Students)

- PLUS Loans must be repaid
- Lender: Banks, credit unions, savings and loans
- Insurance: Insured by lender and re-insured by the state and federal government
- Interest Rate: Variable. Three-month Treasury Bill rate plus 3.1% adjusted annually; cannot exceed 10% (1992-93 rate was 7.36%). Unsubsidized; accrues interest while student is in school
- Deadlines: Apply as soon after January 1st as possible

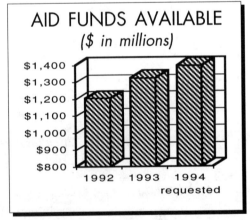

PLUS is an acronym for Parents' Loans for Undergraduate Students, and PLUS lenders are financial institutions such as banks or credit unions. Money for PLUS Loans comes from the same institutions that provide funds for the Stafford Loan program. However, an important overall distinction must be made between the two loans: a PLUS Loan is paid directly to parents, while the Stafford Loan considers students as the primary borrowers. PLUS lenders loan money to parents who wish to borrow, regardless of need, in order to help them finance a dependent's college education. In 1993, over $1.3 billion was disbursed in PLUS Loans (see figure above).

HOW DO PARENTS DETERMINE THEIR ELIGIBILITY?

- They must have a legal dependent enrolled in school at least half-time
- They must be the legal guardians or natural or adoptive parents of the student receiving aid
- They must not have defaulted on any previous student loans
- They must undergo a credit check to determine approval rating
- Parents and dependent students must be U.S. citizens or permanent U.S. residents

GETTING STARTED

Prior to requesting a PLUS application from the financial aid office at your college or university, it is important that you have applied for *all* other available aid. With the PLUS loan, interest starts accumulating following disbursement, and your parents will begin repayment on the loan sixty days after it has been issued. Contact your state's guarantee agency (page 56) and ask for the names of lenders in your area. You may also want to contact your own bank to determine whether they issue PLUS loans. Upon finding a lender, it's important to ask about the insurance fee (usually 3%) charged by many lenders. After your parents have carefully completed the application, return it promptly to the financial aid office. They will fill out their part and transfer it to your lender for processing. Final approval is given by the lender, and it usually takes between five and ten business days to process the application.

Remember, the college or university you're attending determines the amount you can ultimately receive through the PLUS Loan program. Your school has the authority to certify a loan for a smaller amount than you're eligible to receive, or they may even refuse to accept your application.

HOW MUCH CAN I GET?

The amount of money your parents can borrow through the PLUS Loan Program is unlimited as long as they meet all the loan requirements. They can receive enough money to cover the entire cost of your education minus any other federal student aid you have already received.

```
  Cost of your education
- Federal aid already received
= TOTAL PLUS LOAN AMOUNT
```

For loans disbursed on or before July 1, 1993

- $4,000 per year per student
- $20,000 maximum for each dependent student

PAYMENT

If your PLUS loan was first disbursed on or after October 1, 1992, the electronic transfer of funds can make payment easy. After your parents have signed a promissory note, the lender sends a check by computer, made payable to both your school and your parents, to the financial aid office. This speeds up the entire disbursement process and saves you from waiting for loan payment by mail. Payments will be made to your parents at least twice during the year, and if the lender agrees your parents may receive them every week or month. The total amount of each disbursement will never be more than half of the entire amount of the loan and it will always be paid in equal installments.

QUICK TIP: There is no 30-day waiting period for first time PLUS Loan borrowers. Payment is received immediately, according to the school's financial aid disbursement methods.

PAYBACK

Interest

PLUS Loans first disbursed on or after October 1, 1992, have a variable interest rate set each year in June, with a ten percent cap. The organization carrying your loan must notify you of the new rate. The new rate, set on June 30, 1993, is 6.64 %. If you have a PLUS loan that was disbursed to you before that date, contact your lender for the current interest rate. Along with the interest and principal payments, parents must also pay a 5% "origination fee" for loans disbursed after the above date. This fee and the insurance premium (up to 3%) collected by the lender will be deducted from each disbursement in equal amounts.

Installments

With the PLUS Loan program, *there is no grace period before repayment begins* because interest starts accumulating immediately. Your parents have only 60 days from when the loan is first disbursed to begin making a minimum payment of $50 a month. If the loan is sold during the process of repayment, your parents will be notified by both the old and new organizations and given new payment instructions.

This chart shows the approximate repayment schedule for your parents over a five- and ten-year period. All three amounts have an interest rate of 10% (the highest rate possible).

Loan Amount	# of Payments	Monthly	Total Repaid
$2,500	60 (over 5 years)	$51.90	$3,114.00
$4,000	120 (over 10 years)	$52.87	$6,344.00
$7,500	120 (over 10 years)	$99.12	$11,894.40

QUICK TIP: If a PLUS borrower is convicted of possession or dealing of drugs, their loan will be suspended automatically and immediate repayment of the full amount will be required.

Deferment

Your parents do have the option of applying for a deferment with the PLUS Loan program. Deferments apply only to the principal balance of the loan, not the interest. If your parents are granted deferment, they will most likely have to continue making monthly interest payments. Some organizations carrying loans will allow borrowers to postpone interest payments until deferment ends, but this increases the amount of the principal balance. To apply for deferment, you must contact the agency that is carrying your loan. Your parent's eligibility for postponement depends on the current status of the loan and the date it was first disbursed.

QUALIFICATIONS FOR LOANS FIRST DISBURSED ON OR AFTER JULY 1, 1993

Deferment is granted for:
• Child's study in a graduate or fellowship program

Up to three years deferment for:
• Parents' economic difficulties

- Parents' inability to find full-time employment

The loan must not be in default for deferment. An application is obtained by the company carrying the loan and resubmitted every 12 months. For borrowers whose loan disbursement occurred before July 1, 1993, check with your lending institution for deferment details and guidelines.

QUICK TIP: *PLUS borrowers who are not eligible for deferment can apply for "forbearance" as long as they are willing to make loan payments, but cannot afford to do so. Contact the organization carrying your loan for more information.*

Cancellation/Forgiveness

The repayment of a PLUS loan can be cancelled or forgiven, but only under very specific circumstances. If your parents meet the following qualifications, contact the company that carries your loan for cancellation details.
100% forgiveness:
- Bankruptcy (in some cases)
- Complete and permanent disability of the borrower
- Death of the borrower

QUICK TIP: *The Department of Defense may repay a portion of your parent's PLUS Loan as an incentive for you to enlist. Contact a local recruiting officer for more information.*

Any questions you have concerning repayment, deferment, cancellation, or interest rates of your PLUS Loan should be directed to the organization carrying your loan.

SLS (Supplemental Loans for Students)

- SLS loans must be repaid
- Lender: banks, credit unions, savings and loans
- Insurance: Insured by the lender and then re-insured by both the state and federal government
- Interest rate: Variable. Three-month Treasury Bill rate plus 3.1% adjusted annually; cannot exceed 11% (1992-1993 rate was 7.36%). Unsubsidized; accrues interest while student is in school
- Deadlines: Apply as soon after January 1st as possible

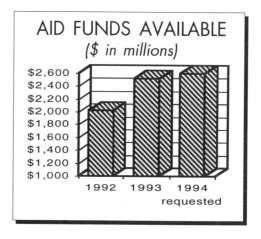

SLS is an acronym for Supplemental Loans for Students. As with both the Stafford and PLUS Loans, money for this type of loan comes from independent financial institutions and is used for educational expenses. And, like PLUS Loan applicants, SLS applicants do not need to show any financial need. In 1993, approximately $2.4 billion was loaned to SLS applicants (see figure above).

HOW DO I DETERMINE MY ELIGIBILITY?

- You must be attending school at least half-time, as an undergraduate or graduate student
- The school of enrollment must qualify as a recipient. If your school's default rate is thirty percent or higher, you are ineligible
- You must have already applied for a Stafford Loan and Pell Grant
- You must be approved for credit by a lending institution
- You must not have previously defaulted on, or currently be in default of, any other student financial loan
- You must be a U.S. citizen or permanent resident
- Programs for study abroad qualify if academic credit is simultaneously earned from a U.S. institution
- You must be legally independent (unless your financial aid advisor rules that you are dependent, with exceptional circumstances)

GETTING STARTED

An SLS applicant follows the same procedures as a Stafford or PLUS Loan applicant. In most cases, you will have to request an SLS application from the financial aid office at your college or university. It is important that you have applied for *all* other available aid (that is, Pell Grant, Perkins Loan, Stafford Loan, or College Work Study) before applying for an SLS Loan, because interest starts accumulating immediately after disbursement and repayment begins 60 days later. Once you've decided to apply for an SLS Loan, contact the loan agency in your state to find a lender in your area. Be sure to check with your bank first because they may provide SLS Loans. Don't forget to ask about an insurance fee (usually 3%) charged by many lenders. After you find a lender, return your completed application to either that office or the school and it will be sent for you. Make sure that your college or university has filled out its section, certifying your registration, the amount of financial aid you will be receiving, and the total cost of your education. The length of the application process differs with every lending institution, but it usually takes between 5 and 10 business days to complete.

Before you receive an SLS Loan, your school will automatically evaluate your eligibility for either a Pell Grant or Stafford Loan. If you qualify for either program, the amount of money you'll receive from the SLS Loan will be less. The college or university you attend determines the amount of money you are able to receive, so your school can certify a loan for a smaller amount than you're eligible for, or they may even refuse to certify your application.

HOW MUCH CAN I GET?

As with the majority of other federal loan programs, the amount of money you are granted through the SLS program depends on your year in school, the amount of money you have already borrowed from the program, and your enrollment status. The following figures show the maximum amount anyone can receive annually:

- First and second year undergraduate students: up to $4,000
- Third and fourth year undergraduate students: up to $5,000
  Maximum amount = $23,000 for undergraduate study
- Graduate and professional study: up to $10,000
  Maximum amount = $73,000 for undergraduate and graduate study combined

These limits apply only to loans made on or after July 1, 1993. If you do not fit into this category, contact the financial aid office at your college or university for the correct figures. Undergraduates attending school less than half-time also are eligible to apply for an SLS Loan. Students may not borrow more than the cost of tuition and educational expenses, minus any other financial aid already received. Also, borrowers can receive only one SLS Loan during a single academic year or over a seven-month period, whichever is longer.

PAYMENT

SLS Loan funds are transferred directly from the lending institution to the school and are then made payable to the borrower through direct payment or by crediting the student's account (or both). As an SLS Loan borrower, you will sign a promissory note, after which you'll receive at least two payments (three on the quarter system or two on the semester system). Students studying overseas will most likely be paid directly in one installment. Payments can also be disbursed once a week or month, depending upon the needs of the lender. In any case, payments are made in equal installments and no payment will ever exceed one-half of the total loan amount.

First-year undergraduate students borrowing an SLS Loan for the first time must wait thirty days after the beginning of school before receiving their first payment. This also applies to any first-time borrower attending a college or university with a default rate over thirty percent. Contact your financial aid office to see if your school falls into this category. Make sure that during this waiting period you have other funds to cover your expenses until you receive your first installment. Emergency loans are usually granted to students who have not yet received their financial aid. Check with your college or university for loan detail and application deadlines (page 48 for more emergency loan information).

PAYBACK

Interest

SLS Loans first disbursed on or after October 1, 1992 have a variable interest rate set every year in June, with an eleven percent cap. The interest rate set June 30, 1993, is 6.64%. The organization carrying your loan is obligated to inform you of the new rate. If you have an SLS Loan that was disbursed to you before the above date, contact your lender for the current interest rate.

QUICK TIP: *Remember that SLS Loans are unsubsidized, meaning that the government does not make interest payments for students while they are in school. Interest begins accumulating immediately.*

In addition to the interest and principal payments, students must also pay an "origination fee" for SLS Loans disbursed on or after October 1, 1992. The five percent fee, along with the insurance premium (up to three percent) collected by the lender, will be deducted equally from each disbursement.

Installments

There is no grace period with an SLS Loan. Borrowers must begin repayment sixty days after the final loan disbursement. Repayment is made monthly to the organization carrying your loan. If your loan is sold to another company, both the old and new organizations must notify you and provide information on where to send payments.

QUICK TIP: If you have both an SLS Loan and a Stafford Loan, you can begin repayment on your SLS at the same time you begin repayment on your Stafford Loan (that is, six months following graduation, leaving school, or other changes in enrollment status). Interest on your SLS Loan still accumulates during this time.

The following chart gives an approximate example of a repayment schedule over a five- and ten- year period with an interest rate of 11% (the highest rate possible).

Loan Amount	# of Payments	Monthly	Total Repaid
$2,500	60 (over 5 years)	$54.37	$3,262.20
$5,000	120 (over 10 years)	$68.88	$8,265.60
$12,500	120 (over 10 years)	$172.20	$20,664.00

QUICK TIP: If your SLS Loan was first granted on or after July 1, 1993, you have a new repayment option. Repayment can be made on an "income-contingency" basis, meaning your financial income will determine the amount of your monthly payments.

DEFERMENT

Most SLS Loan borrowers still enrolled in school are eligible for deferment. Deferring or postponing payments on these loans applies only to the principal balance, not the interest. Some organizations will let the interest accumulate during the deferment period instead of having the borrower make payments. To apply for deferment, you must contact the agency that carries your loan. Deferments must be renewed, usually every twelve months. Your eligibility for deferment depends on the current status of your loan, and the date your loan was first disbursed.

Qualifications for loans first disbursed on or after July 1, 1993

Deferment is granted for:
- Half- to full-time enrollment at a college or university
- Graduate or fellowship study

Up to three years deferment is granted for:
- Economic difficulties
- Inability to find full-time employment

To be considered for deferment, your loan must not be in default. For borrowers whose loan disbursement occurred before July 1, 1993, check with your lending institution for deferment details and guidelines.

FORBEARANCE

SLS borrowers who are not eligible for deferment can apply for "forbearance," as long as they are willing to make loan payments but cannot afford to do so. Forbearance is a period of time when the borrower is not required to make any payments on the interest or principal balance of the loan. To apply, contact the organization that carries your loan. You will be required to present a written statement explaining why you are unable to meet monthly costs.

CANCELLATION/FORGIVENESS

The repayment of an SLS loan may be cancelled or forgiven only under the following specific conditions:

100% forgiveness:

- Bankruptcy (in some cases)
- Complete and permanent disability of the borrower
- Death of the borrower

If you have any questions about repayment, cancellation, deferment, or interest rates for your SLS loan, you should contact the organization holding your loan.

Perkins Loans

- Perkins Loans must be repaid
- Lender: This is a campus-based program with the school acting as the lender
- Insurance: The school insures the loan
- Interest rate: Annual rate of 5%. Usually subsidized; the school makes the determination
- Deadlines: Apply as early in the year as your school allows (usually this is shortly after January 1)

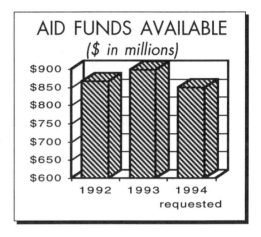

Undergraduate and graduate students who have established financial need may be eligible to receive a Perkins Loan. The Perkins Loan program is commonly referred to as a campus-based program because the schools act as lenders and financial administrators. However, loan dollars actually come from the government. In 1993, over $900 million was distributed through this very low-interest loan program, and priority went to those with the most urgent need. If you are a student who has already been awarded a Pell Grant, your chances of receiving more money from a Perkins Loan are very good.

HOW DO I DETERMINE MY ELIGIBILITY?

- You must be an undergraduate or graduate student
- Your school must have funds allocatable to the Perkins Loan program
- You must be attending school at least half-time
- You must be working on first undergraduate or graduate degree (people working on their second degree are not eligible)

GETTING STARTED

Remember, this is a campus-based loan program, so applicants need to apply at their school (not with an independent lender). As soon as you know that you will be applying for aid, you should visit your financial aid advisor and obtain the FAF or AFSA (see samples starting on page 155). Timeliness is important. Schools cannot give out any more money once they run out, so apply very early for the Perkins Loan. Typically, schools ask that you apply as soon after the first of the year as possible. Proving financial need is also important, so sit down and talk with your financial advisor and your parents to help you determine the best ways to prove need.

HOW MUCH CAN I GET?

- $3,000 per year for undergraduate students, with a maximum of $15,000
- $5,000 per year for graduate students, with a maximum of $30,000 (this figure includes all money from any previous Perkins Loans as well)
- Students may be able to borrow more than the set amount, but only if their school has a default rate of 7.5% or less. Check with the financial aid office at your institution
- Students can borrow up to 20% above the set limit annually if they are participating in a study-abroad program and receiving approved credits from a U.S. institution

PAYMENT

The total amount that your school awards you is dependent on both your financial need and how much money you've received from other aid programs. Once you have qualified for the Perkins Loan, you will need to sign a promissory note to receive your money. A promissory note is a binding agreement between you and the school, stating that you will repay the money you have borrowed. When disbursements are made, the school will either give you the money or credit your account, depending on the system used by the financial aid office. The number of loan payments you receive each year depends on the amount borrowed and your school's operating system. If your school is on the semester system, you'll receive the loan in two payments at the beginning of each semester. Schools running on the quarter system disburse loans at the beginning of each quarter, or at least three times a year. Students who borrow $500 or less for the entire school year will most likely receive only one payment. Every school uses a different method for disbursing aid, so check with the financial aid office at your college or university for details on disbursement dates, times, and locations.

PAYBACK

Installments

The payback plan for the Perkins Loan includes a long grace period for borrowers. A grace period is the time following graduation, termination of studies, or dropping below half-time status, during which students do not have to make payments on their loan balance. Students have nine months before repayment begins with the Perkins Loan. Grace periods vary from school to school in cases where students drop below half-time. Contact the financial aid office for the exact amount of time given to such students.

At the end of the grace period, students begin making monthly payments to their school. The amount of each payment depends on the amount of the loan, the length of the repayment period, and the date the loan was made.

- Loans disbursed before October 1, 1992: payments will be at least $30 a month
- Loans disbursed on or after October 1, 1992: payments will be at least $40 a month

Interest

The interest rate is fixed at 5% and does not accrue until you start making payments. The outstanding balance can be paid once or over ten years. The following chart shows an approximate repayment schedule of three different loan amounts over the maximum ten-year payback period.

Loan Amount	# of Payments	Monthly Payment	Total Repaid
$3,000	120	$31.84	$3,817.86
$5,000	120	$53.06	$6,363.40
$15,000	120	$159.16	$19,090.85

Missed payments, late payments, and payments of less than the full amount are subject to penalty in the form of a late charge, or collection fees. Charges on late payments are determined by each institution on an individual basis and will continue until payments are made on time.

DEFERMENT

Deferring or postponing loan repayments is only granted under specific conditions. To postpone payments, you must fill out a deferment request form, available from the financial aid office at your school. Make sure you file your request before the deadline set by your school or you will be charged a late fee. Your deferment eligibility depends on the date your loan was first disbursed, and the following criteria:

Loans made on or after July 1, 1993

Deferment is granted if you:

- Are enrolled at least half-time at a post-secondary institution
- Are involved in a rehabilitation program for the physically challenged
- Are participating in a graduate fellowship program
- Are serving in the Armed Forces in areas of immediate danger
- Teach full-time (specific qualifications and areas only)
- Volunteer in VISTA or the Peace Corps
- Work as a law enforcement or corrections officer
- Work full-time as a nurse or medical technician
- Work full-time as a public service employee

Deferment may be granted up to three years for:

- Inability to find full-time employment
- Economic difficulties

If your loan was made before July 1, 1993, contact the agency that carries your loan for deferment qualification.

If you need to apply for deferment and meet any one of the preceding qualifications, contact your financial aid office immediately for application details and deadlines. This will prevent you from missing or making any late payments and help you avoid collection fees and late charges.

FORBEARANCE

Any students with loan debts of twenty percent or more of their gross income must be granted forbearance by their loaning institutions. Forbearance is a period in which borrowers do not have to make any interest or principal payments on their loans for up to three years. Students must apply each year through their school to receive this benefit. Forbearance is also granted to students who cannot make payments and are not eligible for loan deferment. Contact the financial aid office at your college or university for application information.

CANCELLATION/FORGIVENESS

Cancellation or forgiveness of a Perkins Loan occurs when the amount owed by the borrower is reduced or credited under certain conditions. Any student who has a Perkins Loan is eligible to apply for cancellation if they choose to work in a specific profession, join the armed forces, or volunteer for certain organizations following graduation. Partial or complete forgiveness depends on the time commitment of the borrower (that is, the more time given, the more money credited). You can request cancellation through your institution under the following conditions:

All Perkins Loans

UP TO 50% FORGIVENESS

- Armed forces service while stationed in areas of immediate danger

UP TO 70% FORGIVENESS

- Peace Corps or VISTA volunteer

100% FORGIVENESS

- Complete and permanent disability of the borrower (100%)
- Bankruptcy (in some cases)
- Death of the borrower (100%)
- Teaching full-time in an area serving low-income students
- Teaching special education or disabled students full-time
- Working as a Head Start Program employee
- Working full-time as a medical technician or nurse

Loans made on or After July 23, 1992

UP TO 100% FORGIVENESS

- Full-time provider of certain services for the physicallychallenged
- Public service employee for child or family agencies in low-income areas
- Teaching full-time in an area where there is a shortage of teachers

Loans made on or after November 29, 1990

UP TO 100% FORGIVENESS

- Full-time service as a corrections or law enforcement officer

QUICK TIP: *If you serve in a certain selected division of the Armed Forces, the Department of Defense may repay a portion of your Perkins Loan as an incentive for you to enlist. Contact a local recruiting officer for more information.*

If you would like to apply for cancellation and you meet any one of the preceding requirements, contact your institution for application details.

Remember, any questions or concerns you may have about deferments, repayment schedules, cancellations, or borrower responsibilities of your Perkins Loan must be directed to the financial aid office at the school where the loan was granted.

Any student eligible for a loan through either a federal or private program needs to know the rights and responsibilities that come with borrowing money to finance an education. These guidelines are established to protect you, the student, and to make sure you fully understand the conditions of each individual loan.

When you receive your first loan disbursement, you will be required to sign a promissory note. This note is a binding legal agreement and, by signing, you agree to repay the loan in full according to the terms stated in the note. Even if you do not finish school or are unable to find employment after graduation, you must pay back the entire amount of the loan. During the repayment period, you continue to make payments whether or not you receive a billing statement. Remember to notify the organization carrying your loan if you move, change your name, or if your enrollment status changes. If you have applied for a deferment, make sure that you continue to make payments until the deferment is processed. By not following these obligations, there is a chance that your loan may end up in default.

It's important that, as a borrower, you not only are aware of your obligations, but also of your rights. You are entitled to an approximate loan repayment schedule which should include the amount, number, and exact date of all your loan payments. If your loan repayment schedule includes a grace period, you have a right to that entire length of time before your repayment commences. You should also be informed of the deferment and cancellation conditions, details, and application procedures.

Borrower Rights and Responsibilities

Prior to receiving your first loan disbursement, the college or university you attend and the organization that is carrying your loan must inform you of the following information in the entrance interview:

- The total amount of the loan you are borrowing and the current interest rate charges
- Information on extra charges (that is, origination fee and insurance): when and how they will be collected from you
- The maximum amount of money that can be borrowed each year through the program
- Time allotted for repayment
- A current statement of loans already owed
- An example of a monthly repayment schedule and an estimate of the total amount that will be owed
- How borrowing will affect your eligibility to receive other forms of aid
- The date you must begin repayment of your loan
- Loan consolidation and prepayment options
- An explanation of "defaulting" on a loan

Following graduation or the completion of your studies, you must be given an exit interview by your college or university and/or the company that is carrying your loan. In this interview, you should receive the following information:

- The total amount of the money you owe
- The current interest rate and all accumulated interest charges owed
- Amount of approximate monthly payments
- Any extra charges or fees that may appear on your monthly statement
- All the information needed about the organization that is carrying your loan
- Repayment management skills and advice
- Deferment, default, and cancellation guidelines
- Consolidation, repayment, and refinancing options

HOW TO BE A RESPONSIBLE BORROWER

The key to being a responsible borrower is organization. By staying organized, you'll be able to keep track of all your student loan information and, most importantly, make your payments on time!

- Make copies of everything. This includes loan applications, promissory notes, statements, and any other important documentation.

- Never throw away anything that has to do with your loan. This includes cancelled checks, and notification your loan has been sold to another organization.

- Keep all of your student loan information in one safe place. File folders, binders, or drawers work well.

- Make a yearly calendar of loan-payment due dates and when to send them.

- If you change your address, notify your lender immediately.

- If you are having trouble meeting your payments, contact your lender immediately for information on other repayment options. These include deferment, forbearance, consolidation, or reduced payments.

Loan Defaults

When you sign a promissory note, you are agreeing to repay all the money you borrowed through these higher education loan programs. A promissory note is a binding legal document stating the amount of money you are borrowing and the terms under which the loan is to be repaid. Repayment on almost all of the federal and state student loans begins after the borrower has graduated from college or drops below half-time enrollment status. A grace period follows a change of student status; this is a specific time period before loan repayment begins. Most grace periods last between six and twelve months, depending on interest rates and the type of loan(s) borrowed. The following time periods correspond to these individual loans:

PERIOD LENGTHS

Perkins Loans
- Nine months

Stafford Loans (subsidized)
- 8% interest or more - six months
- 7% interest or less- nine to twelve months

PLUS, SLS, Stafford Loans (unsubsidized)
- Repayment starts sixty days after loan disbursement

These grace periods give students time to organize finances and find a job after graduation.

At the end of the grace period, if the agency has not already contacted them, students are responsible for contacting the agency carrying their loan to inquire about repayment schedules and methods. Loan payments are usually made on a monthly or quarterly basis. As a borrower, you are responsible for making these payments on time. If you are very late or fail to make payments, your loan will become delinquent. Delinquency is defined as "failing to make loan payments when they are due," and your loan will remain in this state until the overdue balance is settled or other arrangements (such as deferment) are made.

QUICK TIP: *Almost all lending institutions are willing to make alternative payment plans if you are having trouble meeting your repayment schedule. If you foresee financial difficulty, contact the agency carrying your loan immediately to explain your situation. Do not just skip a payment without explanation because you don't have the funds to cover it.*

If monthly payments are delinquent for six months (180 days), or quarterly payments have not been made for eight months (240 days), your account is then in default. Once a loan is in default, it is purchased by a credit agency which collects the loan money directly from you. Borrowers who allow their loans to reach this state are subject to the following restrictions:

• Borrowers will no longer be eligible to receive any state or federal financial aid assistance

• The loan(s) will be referred to a collection agency

• Loan payments may be deducted from your paychecks

• The IRS may hold your tax refund and use it for loan payment

• Because default affects credit rating it will be difficult to be approved for car and house loans or establish other forms of credit

• Borrowers are subject to possible legal action for retrieval of payment

• Borrowers are ineligible for deferment or forgiveness of the loan balance

There are several options to prevent you from defaulting on your loan(s). Guarantee agencies offer borrowers the chance to defer payments for financial hardship and other reasons, and there are even situations in which a portion of your loan balance may be forgiven (see page 56). Keep your loan agency informed of your financial situation and it will work with you to prevent delinquency or default.

LOAN CONSOLIDATION

Loan consolidation is another repayment option for students with multiple outstanding loans and, together with deferment and forgiveness, it can help you avoid default or delinquency. If you borrowed money from several different state and federal loan programs to cover the cost of your education, you may be able to "consolidate" those loans into one. Consolidating your loans will most likely lower your monthly payments and make the repayment process simpler because you only make one monthly payment.

QUICK TIP: *By consolidating your loans, your repayment period can be extended from 10 years to a maximum of 25 years, depending on the total amount of your debt. Contact the agency that carries your loan for more information on consolidation.*

Eligibility for the Loan Consolidation Program depends on the amount you owe and the types of loans you have received. Students must have borrowed at least $5,000 from one or more of these programs:

• Health Professions Student Loans (HPLS)

• Perkins Loans

• Stafford Loans

• SLS Loans

The interest rate on consolidated loans is usually 9%, unless your loan agency takes the interest rate on all of your loans, adds them together, and takes the higher average. The total amount you owe, rates, and the amount of your monthly payments are to be determined by the agency that carries your loans.

To consolidate your loans, you must have begun to make payments or be in the grace period before repayment begins. Borrowers who are more than ninety days delinquent in payments or are in default, will not qualify for this program. If you are eligible for and interested in consolidation, contact your lending agency to tell them how much you owe on your loans and the kinds of loans you have. If you have Stafford or Perkins Loans, the agency will purchase them from the federal government and handle all collection and payment methods.

Emergency Loans

Almost every college and university offers its students some type of *temporary* loan assistance. Each institution has either an Emergency Loan Department or Office of Student Accounts in which the school acts as a direct lender to students in need. Emergency loans are interest-free or have low interest rates. These loans are granted to half-time or full-time students who are unable to meet education-related expenses.

Funds are available to students for:

•   Tuition

•   Rent

•   Books and supplies

•   Miscellaneous costs

These loans are also granted to students who have applied for, but have not yet received, financial aid. It's important to remember that you're responsible for tuition payment and other school-related expenses even if your financial aid has not been disbursed. Undergraduates who are first-time federal loan borrowers must wait thirty days following the beginning of classes to receive their money. In these cases, your school will loan you the funds to cover these costs until your aid arrives. Once your aid is disbursed, most schools will deduct the amount of your emergency loan from your principal financial aid balance.

Applying for an emergency loan is a simple process at almost every institution. Generally, each application takes only about five to ten minutes to complete and three to five days to process. Usually, the only information required for these forms is your name, address, student identification number, two or three references, and a general explanation of your need. Most schools charge a processing fee that is added to the principal balance and due when the loan is repaid. The fee differs at each institution, but averages between $5 and $20.

QUICK TIP: *When applying for an emergency loan, make sure you allow enough time for the form to be processed so that you will receive the money in time to pay your bills. Check with the financial aid office at your school for the length of the processing period.*

Emergency loans are granted immediately, without question, unless the student has an unpaid balance or has previously defaulted on an emergency loan. The amount of money each student is eligible to receive depends on the student's expenses. Most schools have a set amount for tuition and other expenses, but students are eligible to borrow more than this amount with a co-signer. The co-signer can be a parent, legal guardian, or responsible adult who signs a promissory note agreeing to fully repay the amount borrowed. Students usually have between three and six months to repay the loan, depending on the institution. If you can't meet the deadline, most schools will grant extensions depending on your financial situation.

Remember that your college or university is willing to help you in any way possible. If you are having or anticipate having difficulty meeting your tuition, living, or other expenses, contact the financial aid office at your school for information on emergency loans.

Planning for the Future

Almost every student is eligible for some type of free aid, either in the form of grants or scholarships, but this isn't always enough to cover rising college costs. After you have applied for and received all possible free aid, it's time to take out a student loan to meet the rest of your educational expenses. Federal and state governments have devised a guaranteed student loan program which allows students to borrow money at a low interest rate to make up the difference that free aid can't cover. Before you decide to borrow money, there are a few important issues to consider:

- What are the interest charges?
- How long do I have to repay the loan?
- What is the minimum payment required per month?
- Will my income after college cover all of my expenses, including loan payments?
- Does repayment begin during or after college?

At the time of disbursement, loans may seem like free money since repayment is not required immediately. However, it is important to remember that, eventually, you will have to repay all the money you've borrowed, plus interest.

To avoid unwanted debt after college, the best thing to do before you decide to borrow money is to seriously consider your financial position and evaluate your future income and expenses following graduation. This may be difficult, but it could prevent you from extending yourself beyond your financial means. To financially plan your future, you need to estimate the total cost of your education (see page 51) and the amount of money you expect to earn after graduation in your chosen profession. You must then deduct your cost of living to determine how much money you have left for monthly loan repayments:

Typical Student Expenses

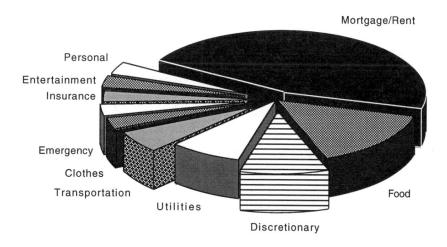

AVERAGE YEARLY INCOME FOR ENTRY LEVEL POSITIONS

To help you plan ahead, complete the sample budget on the following page, taking into account your estimated income and all of your monthly expenses. Use the following list of average starting salaries for your approximate income. If you are unsure of your occupation, use the "average income figure" salary of a four-year college graduate.

Two- and Four-Year Degree	Per Month	Annual
Accountant	$1,700	$20,400
Advertising	$1,700	$20,400
Architecture	$1,916	$22,990
Barber/Hair Stylist	$1,166	$13,990
Broadcast Journalism	$1,000	$12,000
Business	$1,500	$18,000
Buyer	$1,725	$20,700
Carpenter	$1,300	$15,600
Chemist	$1,950	$23,400
Communications	$1,275	$15,300
Computer Programmer	$2,500	$30,000
Cosmetology	$1,000	$12,000
Dental Assistant	$954	$11,450
Editor	$2,000	$24,000
Electronic Technician	$1,500	$18,000
Engineer	$2,481	$29,770
Finance	$1,480	$17,760
Health Technician	$1,225	$14,700
Hotel Management	$1,833	$22,000
Human Resources	$1,833	$22,000
Law Enforcement	$1,675	$20,100
Lawyer	$1,875	$22,500
Marketing	$1,480	$17,760
Medical Assistant	$833	$10,000
Mechanic	$1,170	$14,040
Nurse	$1,666	$19,990
Office Work (general)	$997	$11,940
Plumber	$1,700	$20,400
Public Relations	$1,748	$20,980
Secretary	$1,500	$18,000
Social Worker	$1,391	$16,690
Teacher (secondary)	$1,600	$19,200
Telemarketing	$1,833	$22,000
2nd Lieutenant (Army)	$1,500	$18,000
Average Income (four-year college graduate)	$1,500	$18,000

MONTHLY EXPENSE WORKSHEET

EXPECTED ANNUAL INCOME: $ _____
      Taxes (about 25%)   − _____
      Net Income (divide by 12)   = _____
      Net Monthly Income $ _____

LIVING EXPENSES

1. Rent or Mortgage Payments $ _____

2. Furniture/Appliances   + _____

3. Insurance (fire, renters, etc.)   + _____

4. Utilities
      Phone $ _____
      Heat   + _____
      Electricity   + _____
      Water   + _____
      Other   + _____
Total Utilities   + _____

5. Food
      Grocery Shopping $ _____
      Eating Out   + _____
      Snacks   + _____
      Other   + _____
Total Food   + _____

6. Clothing
      New Clothes $ _____
      Dry Cleaning   + _____
      Laundry   + _____
      Other   + _____
Total Clothing   + _____

7. Personal
      Haircuts $ _____
      Cosmetics   + _____
      Emergency Money   + _____
      Entertainment   + _____
      Other   + _____
Total Personal   + _____

8. Medical Bills
    Doctor $ _____
    Dental   + _____
    Prescriptions   + _____
    Insurance   + _____
    Other   + _____
Total Medical Bills   + _____

9. Car & Transportation
    Car Payments $ _____
    Car Maintenance   + _____
    Insurance   + _____
    Gas (monthly)   + _____
    Airline Tickets   + _____
    Other   + _____
Total Car & Transportation   + _____

10. LOAN REPAYMENTS
    Student Loans $ _____
    Credit Cards   + _____
    Other   + _____
TOTAL LOAN REPAYMENTS   + _____

TOTAL MONTHLY EXPENSES   = _____

State Aid Programs

Student Financial Services

State Aid

All states have established their own higher educational assistance programs which can supplement Federal Aid programs. In 1991-1992, states offered $1,724,934,000 in awards for need-based scholarships and grants (see map on next page). The aid programs themselves are quite varied. To simplify things, we have provided you with a complete and up-to-date phone list of state agencies which you can contact for information on eligibility requirements.

When you call your state educational assistance office, ask for the following:

- Financial aid handbook (or something similar) that gives details on state loans, grants, and other aid programs plus the criteria used to determine your eligibility

- A breakdown of the different state programs so that you can begin thinking about what programs may be of interest to you

- Copies of all the application forms that you will need to apply for state aid programs (be greedy; if you have all the forms now, you won't have to seek them out later)

- Suggestions as to how you can speed up the application process

- Application deadlines

Many state aid programs are available to both those in need of coverage for all expenses and those who need only partial assistance. For instance, if you are in the top ten percent of your graduating class, having maintained a high degree of academic achievement, you may be eligible for state scholarship programs regardless of your financial need. Along the same lines, states today are providing more and more aid to people who intend to go into teaching, nursing, or social services within their own state. Every state has its programs, and every program has its own eligibility requirements. Information that you receive from the state educational aid office, coupled with advice from your school's financial aid office and/or guidance counselor, should start you going in the right direction.

With informational assistance from each state, we have compiled a list of more than 450 scholarships offered through each state's higher education agency. This list includes the amount, deadline, and requirements, and represents only a fraction of the scholarships and grants that are available to state residents and students who are pursuing a degree at a state or private institution. Even students who are not residents of the state in which they are studying may be eligible for some of these financial awards. The application process differs in every state. To be considered for these scholarships students may be required to complete either the AFSA, FAF, or an individual application for state aid. Review the list of scholarships provided (page 62), and contact your state agency for more information. Use the state phone list on the following pages to find the phone number for your state agencies.

QUICK TIP: *One of the things that may determine your eligibility for state aid and the amount of tuition you pay is whether you are a resident of the state in which you are studying. Becoming a resident in a particular state usually entails residing and working in the state anywhere from six to twelve consecutive months. These requirements differ in every state, so contact the financial aid or registrar's office for more information.*

FINANCIAL AWARDS BY STATE

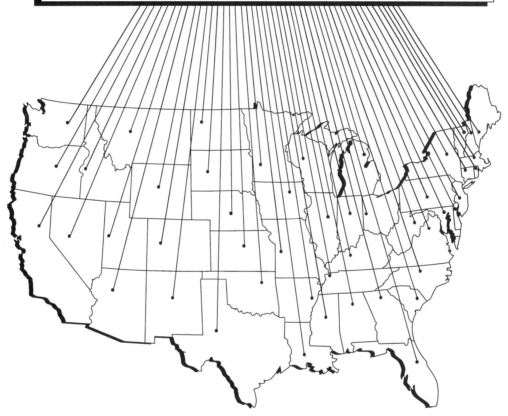

Total 1991-1992 State awards for need-based undergraduate scholarship and grant programs

$1,724,934,000

Awards by state *(in thousands)*

Alabama..... $2,845	Illinois....... $189,607	Montana....... $395	Rhode Island.. $9,672
Alaska......... $471	Indiana...... $50,054	Nebraska..... $2,352	South Carolina. $16,966
Arizona...... $3,311	Iowa....... $34,873	Nevada........ $332	South Dakota.... $480
Arkansas..... $7,083	Kansas....... $6,882	New Hampshire.. $839	Tennessee.... $13,086
California.... $166,236	Kentucky..... $21,075	New Jersey.. $102,290	Texas....... $26,899
Colorado..... $12,430	Louisiana..... $4,717	New Mexico... $7,293	Utah........ $1,042
Connecticut.. $20,467	Maine....... $5,044	New York.... $436,660	Vermont...... $11,129
Delaware..... $1,090	Maryland..... $16,411	North Carolina. $2,758	Virginia....... $7,390
District of Columbia $970	Massachusetts. $23,748	North Dakota.. $1,600	Washington... $23,483
Florida...... $27,159	Michigan..... $78,145	Ohio........ $61,000	West Virginia. $5,806
Georgia...... $4,804	Minnesota.... $77,678	Oklahoma.... $12,751	Wisconsin..... $42,595
Hawaii........ $661	Mississippi..... $1,175	Oregon...... $11,852	Wyoming....... $220
Idaho......... $370	Missouri...... $10,125	Pennsylvania. $158,613	

STATE AGENCIES LISTING

ALABAMA
Stafford/PLUS/SLS/State Aid
Alabama Commission on Higher
Education
3465 Norman Bridge Road
Montgomery, AL 36105
(205) 281-1921

ALASKA
Stafford/PLUS/SLS/State Aid
Alaska Commission on Post-
Secondary Education
3030 Vintage Boulevard
Juneau, AK 99801-7109
(907) 465-2962

ARIZONA
Stafford/PLUS/SLS
Arizona Educational Loan Program
P.O. Box 3028
Chandler, AZ 85244
(800) 352-3033

State Aid
Arizona Commission for Post-
Secondary
Education
2020 North Central Avenue, Suite 275
Phoenix, AZ 85004
(602) 229-2590

ARKANSAS
Stafford/PLUS/SLS
Student Loan Guarantee
Foundation of Arkansas
219 South Victory
Little Rock, AR 72201-1884
(501) 372-1491

State Aid
Department of Higher Education
114 East Capitol
Little Rock, AR 72201
(501) 324-9300

CALIFORNIA
Stafford/PLUS/SLS/State Aid
California Student Aid Commission
P.O. Box 510845
Sacramento, CA 94245-0845
(916) 323-0435

COLORADO
Stafford/PLUS/SLS
Colorado Student Loan Program
999-18th Street, Suite 425
Denver, CO 80202
(303) 294-5050

State Aid
Colorado Commission on Higher
Education
Colorado Heritage Center
1300 Broadway, 2nd Floor
Denver, CO 80203
(303) 866-2723

CONNECTICUT
Stafford/PLUS/SLS
Connecticut Student Loan Foundation
P.O. Box 1009
Rocky Hill, CT 06067
(203) 257-4001

State Aid
Connecticut State Department of
Higher Education
61 Woodland Street
Hartford, CT 06105
(203) 566-2618

DELAWARE
Higher Education Loan Program
Carvel State Office Building
820 North French Street, 4th Floor
Wilmington, DE 19801
Stafford/PLUS/SLS
(302) 577-6055
State Aid
(302) 577-3240

DISTRICT OF COLUMBIA
Stafford/PLUS/SLS
American Student Assistance
1413 K Street NW, Suite 900
Washington, DC 20005
(202) 682-1996

State Aid
Office of Post-Secondary Education
Research and Assistance
D.C. Dept. of Human Services
2100 ML King Jr. Avenue SE, Suite 401
Washington, DC 20020
(202) 727-3688

FLORIDA
Office of Student Financial Assistance
2661 Executive Center Circle West
Clifton Building, Room 100
Tallahassee, FL 32301
Stafford/PLUS/SLS
(904) 488-8093
State Aid
(904) 488-6181

GEORGIA

Georgia Student Finance Commission
2082 East Exchange Place, Suite 200
Tucker, GA 30084
Stafford/PLUS/SLS/State Aid
(404) 414-3000

HAWAII

Stafford/PLUS/SLS
Hawaii Education Loan Program
1314 S. King Street, Suite 861
Honolulu, HI 96814
(808) 536-3731

State Aid
State Post-Secondary Education
Commission
2444 Dole Street
Bachmen Hall, Room 209
Honolulu, HI 96822
(808) 956-8213

IDAHO

Stafford/PLUS/SLS
Student Loan Fund of Idaho, Inc.
Processing Center
P.O. Box 1000
Fruitland, ID 83619
(208) 452-4058

State Aid
Office of State Board of Education
650 West State Street, Room 307
Boise, ID 83720
(208) 334-2270

ILLINOIS

Stafford/PLUS/SLS/State Aid
Illinois State Scholarship
Commission
1755 Lake Cook Road
Deerfield, IL 60015
(708) 948-8500

INDIANA

State Student Assistance
Commission of Indiana
Ista Center Building
150 West Market Street, Suite 500
Indianapolis, IN 46204
Stafford/PLUS/SLS
(317) 232-2366
State Aid
(317) 232-2351

IOWA

Iowa College Aid Commission
201 Jewett Building
914 Grand Avenue
Des Moines, IA 50309-2824
Stafford/PLUS/SLS
(515) 281-4890
State Aid
(515) 281-3501

KANSAS

Stafford/PLUS/SLS
USA Services Application Processing
P.O. Box 6180
Indianapolis, IN 46206
(800) 824-7044

State Aid
Kansas Board of Regents
700 South West Harrison, Suite 1410
Topeka, KS 66603
(913) 296-3517

KENTUCKY

Stafford/PLUS/SLS/State Aid
Kentucky Higher Education Authority
1050 U.S. 127 South, Suite 102
Frankfort, KY 40601
(502) 564-7990
(800) 928-8926

LOUISIANA

Stafford/PLUS/SLS/State Aid
Louisiana Office of Student Financial
Assistance
P.O. Box 91202
Baton Rouge, LA 70821-9202
(800) 259-5626

MAINE

Stafford/PLUS/SLS/State Aid
Finance Authority of Maine
Maine Education Assistance Division
State House Station #119
One Weston Court
Augusta, ME 04333
(207) 287-2183

MARYLAND

Stafford/PLUS/SLS
Maryland Higher Education Loan
Corporation
2100 Guilford Avenue, Room 305
Baltimore, MD 21218
(410) 333-6555

State Aid
Maryland Higher Education
Commission
State Scholarship Administration
The Jeffrey Building
16 Francis Street
Annapolis, MD 21401-1781
(410) 974-5370

MASSACHUSETTS

Stafford/PLUS/SLS
American Student Assistance
330 Stuart Street
Boston, MA 02116
(800) 999-9080

State Aid
Massachusetts State Scholarship
Program
330 Stuart Street
Boston, MA 02116
(617) 727-9420

MICHIGAN

Stafford/PLUS/SLS
Michigan Department of Education
Guaranteed Student Loan Program
P.O. Box 30047
Lansing, MI 48909
(517) 373-0760

State Aid
Michigan Department of Education
Office of Student Financial Assistance
P.O. Box 30008
Lansing, MI 48909
(517) 373-3394

MINNESOTA

Stafford/PLUS/SLS
North Star Guarantee
P.O. Box 64102
St. Paul, MN 55164-0102
(612) 227-7661

State Aid
Minnesota Higher Education
Coordinating Board
Capitol Square, Suite 400
550 Cedar Street
St. Paul, MN 55101
(612) 296-3974

MISSISSIPPI

Stafford/PLUS/SLS
Mississippi Guarantee Student Loan
Agency
3825 Ridgewood Road
Jackson, MS 39211
(601) 982-6663

State Aid
Office of State Student Financial Aid
3825 Ridgewood Road
Jackson, MS 39211-6453
(601) 982-6577

MISSOURI

Stafford/PLUS/SLS/State Aid
Coordinating Board for Higher
Education
P.O. Box 6730
Jefferson City, MO 65102
(314) 751-2361

MONTANA

Stafford/PLUS/SLS/State Aid
Montana Guaranteed Student Loan
Program
2500 Broadway
Helena, MT 59620-3103
(406) 444-6594

NEBRASKA

Stafford/PLUS/SLS
Higher Education Loan Program
1300 O Street
Lincoln, NE 68508
(402) 475-7272

State Aid
Coordinating Commission for Post-
Secondary Education
P.O. Box 95005
140 North 8th Street, Suite 300
Lincoln, NE 68509-5005
(402) 471-2847

NEVADA

Stafford/PLUS/SLS
United Student Aid Group
11100 USA Parkway
Fishers, IN 46038
(317) 849-6510

State Aid
University of Nevada-Reno
Student Financial Aid Service-076
Second Floor-TSSC, Room 200
Reno, NV 89557-0065
(702) 784-4666

NEW HAMPSHIRE

Stafford/PLUS/SLS
New Hampshire Higher Education
Assistance Foundation
P.O. Box 877
Concord, NH 03302-0877
(603) 225-6612
(800) 525-2577

State Aid
Post-Secondary Education
Commission
2 Industrial Park Drive
Concord, NH 03301-8512
(603) 271-2555

NEW JERSEY

Stafford/PLUS/SLS
New Jersey Higher Education
Assistance Authority
4 Quakerbridge, CN 543
Trenton, NJ 08625
(609) 588-3200

State Aid
Department of Higher Education
Office of Grants and Scholarships
20 West State Street, CN 542
Trenton, NJ 08625
(800) 792-8670

NEW MEXICO

Stafford/PLUS/SLS
New Mexico Educational Assistance
Foundation
P.O. Box 27020
Albuquerque, NM 87125-7020
(505) 345-3371

State Aid
Commission on Higher Education
1068 Cerrillos Road
Santa Fe, NM 87501-4295
(505) 827-7383

NEW YORK

Higher Education Services
Corporation
99 Washington Avenue
Albany, NY 12255
Stafford/PLUS/SLS
(518) 473-1574
State Aid
(518) 474-5642

NORTH CAROLINA

Stafford/PLUS/SLS/State Aid
North Carolina State Education
Assistance Authority
Box 2688
Chapel Hill, NC 27515-2688
(919) 549-8614

NORTH DAKOTA

Stafford/PLUS/SLS
Bank of North Dakota
Student Loan Department
Box 5509
Bismark, ND 58502-5524
(800) 472-2166

State Aid
Student Financial Assistance Program
North Dakota University System
600 East Boulevard

Bismark, ND 58505-0230
(701) 224-4114

OHIO

Stafford/PLUS/SLS
Ohio Student Loan Commission
P.O. Box 16610
Columbus, OH 43266-0610
(800) 837-6752

State Aid
Student Assistance Office
Ohio Board of Regents
309 South Fourth Street
Columbus, OH 43215
(614) 466-7420

OKLAHOMA

Stafford/PLUS/SLS/State Aid
Oklahoma State Regents for Higher
Education
P.O. Box 3000
Oklahoma City, OK 73101
(800) 442-8642

OREGON

Oregon State Scholarship Commission
1500 Valley River Drive #100
Eugene, OR 97401
(800) 452-8807
Stafford/PLUS/SLS
(503) 687-7375
State Aid
(503) 687-7395

PENNSYLVANIA

Pennsylvania Higher Education
Assistance Agency
1200 North 7th Street
Harrisburg, PA 17102-8172
Stafford/PLUS/SLS
(800) 692-7392
State Aid
(800) 692-7435

RHODE ISLAND

Stafford/PLUS/SLS/State Aid
Rhode Island Higher Education
Assistance
Authority
560 Jefferson Boulevard
Warwick, RI 02886
in state
(401) 736-1100
out of state
(800) 922-9855

59

SOUTH CAROLINA
Stafford/PLUS/SLS
South Carolina Student Loan
Corporation
16 Berryhill Road
Interstate Center, Suite 210
P.O. Box 21487
Columbia, SC 29221
(803) 798-0916

State Aid
South Carolina Tuition Grants
Commission
1310 Lady Street
P.O. Box 12159
Columbia, SC 29211-2159
(803) 734-1200

SOUTH DAKOTA
Stafford/PLUS/SLS
Education Assistance Corporation
115 First Avenue SW
Aberdeen, SD 57401
(605) 225-6423

State Aid
Department of Education and
Cultural Affairs
Richard F. Kneip Building
700 Governors Drive
Pierre, SD 57501-2291
(605) 773-3134

TENNESSEE
Stafford/PLUS/SLS/State Aid
Tennessee Student Assistance
Corporation
Parkway Tower, Suite 1950
404 James Robertson Parkway
Nashville, TN 37243-0820
in state
(800) 342-1663
out of state
(800) 257-6526

TEXAS
Stafford/PLUS/SLS
Texas Guaranteed Student Loan
Corporation
P.O. Box 15996
Austin, TX 78761
(512) 835-1900

State Aid
Texas Higher Education Coordinating
Board
Box 12788
Austin, TX 78711-2788
(800) 242-3062

UTAH
Stafford/PLUS/SLS
Utah Guarantee Agency
P.O. Box 45202
Salt Lake City, UT 84145-0202
(801) 321-7200

State Aid
Utah State Board of Regents
355 West North Temple, Suite 550
Salt Lake City, UT 84180-1205
(801) 321-7100

VERMONT
Stafford/PLUS/SLS/State Aid
Vermont Student Assistance
Corporation
Champlain Mill
P.O. Box 999
Winooski, VT 05404-2601
in state
(800) 642-3177
out of state
(802) 654-3790

VIRGINIA
Stafford/PLUS/SLS
State Education Assistance Authority
One Franklin Square
411 East Franklin Street, Suite 300
Richmond, VA 23219
(804) 775-4000

State Aid
State Council of Higher Education for
Virginia
James Monroe Building
101 North 14th Street, 9th Floor
Richmond, VA 23219
(804) 225-2141

WASHINGTON
Stafford/PLUS/SLS
Northwest Education Loan
Association
811 First Avenue #500
Seattle, WA 98104
(800) 562-3001

State Aid
Higher Education Coordinating Board
P.O. Box 43430
917 Lakeridge Way
Olympia, WA 98504-3430
(206) 753-3571

WEST VIRGINIA

Stafford/PLUS/SLS
West Virginia Education Loan
Services
P.O. Box 591
Kanawha Boulevard East, Suite 310
Charleston, WV 25322-0591
in state
(800) 437-3692
out of state
(304) 345-7211

State Aid
West Virginia Higher Education Grant
Program
P.O. Box 4007
Charleston, WV 25364-4007
(304) 347-1211

WISCONSIN

Stafford/PLUS/SLS
Great Lakes Higher Education
2401 International Lane
Madison, WI 53704
(800) 236-6600

State Aid
Wisconsin Higher Educational Aids
Board
P.O. Box 7885
Madison, WI 53707-7885
(608) 266-1660

WYOMING

Stafford/PLUS/SLS/State Aid
United Student Aid Funds
1912 Capitol Avenue, Suite 320
Cheyenne, WY 82001
(800) 742-9659

GUAM

Educational Loan Program
United Student Aid Funds, Inc.
1314 South King Street, Suite 861
Honolulu, HI 96814
(808) 536-3731

PUERTO RICO

Higher Education Assistance
Corporation
P.O. Box 42001
Minillas Station
San Juan, Puerto Rico 00940-2001
(809) 763-3575

State Scholarship, Grant, and Loan Listings

The following scholarships are listed alphabetically by state. Be certain to check the scholarships for:

- The state in which you have legal residence
- The state of the college you are currently attending
- All of the states you have previously lived in for an extended period of time (including your state of birth).

QUICK TIP: *When an organization has several listings within a state, only the first listing has the address. If you find a state scholarship that you are eligible to apply for and the address is not listed, simply refer to the previous address listed. Make sure to identify the program in which you are interested in your letter of request or application.*

Alabama

Alabama Commission on Higher Education (Alabama G.I. Dependents' Educational Benefit Program)
3465 Norman Bridge Road
Montgomery, AL 36105-2310
Amount: Varies
Deadline: None
College Major: All Majors
Requirements: Applicants must be the spouses or children of eligible Alabama Veterans. To qualify, applicants must be currently enrolled in public post-secondary educational institutions in the state of Alabama. Applications are available from any county veterans service officer.

Alabama Commission on Higher Education (Alabama Junior and Community College Athletic Scholarships)
Amount: Varies
Deadline: None
College Major: All Majors
Requirements: Applicants should be full-time students registered in public junior and community colleges in Alabama. Athletic ability will determine nomination. Grants do not exceed tuition and books for attendance. Contact financial aid officer, coach, or athletic director for applications and more information.

Alabama Commission on Higher Education (Alabama Junior and Community College Performing Arts Scholarships)
Amount: Varies
Deadline: None
College Major: All Majors
Requirements: Applicants must be full-time students enrolled in public junior and community colleges in Alabama. Awards will be given to those with proven talent displayed at competitive auditions. Grants do not surpass in-state tuition for attendance at community colleges or junior colleges in Alabama. Contact financial aid office for applications.

Alabama Commission on Higher Education (Alabama Nursing Scholarship)
Amount: Varies
Deadline: Varies
College Major: Nursing

Requirements: After completion of the nursing program, applicants must consent to practice nursing for at least one year. Applicants must be Alabama residents enrolled at an Alabama institution participating in the nursing program. Contact the financial aid office for an application.

Alabama Commission on Higher Education (Alabama Police Officer's and Firefighter's Survivor's Educational Assistance)
Amount: Varies
Deadline: None
College Major: All Majors
Requirements: Scholarships are available to students who are dependents or spouses of police officers or firefighters killed in the line of duty in Alabama. Applicants must be registered in an undergraduate program at a public post-secondary educational institution in Alabama. Write for application and more information.

Alabama Commission on Higher Education (Alabama Two-Year College Academic Scholarship)
Amount: Varies
Deadline: None
College Major: All Majors
Requirements: Applicants must be attending a two-year post-secondary institution in Alabama. Awards cover tuition and expenses and are renewable on a yearly basis. Contact the financial aid office at your school of study for more information.

Alabama Commission on Higher Education (Emergency Secondary Education Scholarship Program)
Amount: Up to $3996.00
Deadline: June 1
College Major: Education
Requirements: Awards are available to Alabama residents who are currently teaching in Alabama state schools. Funds are to be used to reenter a masters degree program, or obtain certification. Write for more information.

Alabama Commission on Higher Education (National Guard Educational Assistance Program)
Amount: $500.00 to $1000.00
Deadline: None
College Major: All Majors
Requirements: Awards are open to Alabama National Guard members who are Alabama residents. Scholarships are for undergraduate or graduate study. Applicant must be a U.S. citizen or legal resident. Write for more information.

Alabama Commission on Higher Education (Robert C. Byrd Honors Scholarship)
Amount: $1500.00
Deadline: Varies
College Major: All Majors
Requirements: Scholarships are awarded based on academic achievement and show of promise of continued academic achievement. Applications are available from Alabama high school guidance counselors. Write for application and more information

Alabama Commission on Higher Education (Student Assistance Program)
Amount: $3000.00 to $2500.00
Deadline: None
College Major: All Majors
Requirements: Grants are available to undergraduate students at nonprofit Alabama colleges and universities not receiving direct appropriations from the state. Applications are available at participating institutions or write for more information.

Alabama Commission on Higher Education (Student Grant Program)
Amount: Up to $1200.00
Deadline: None
College Major: All Majors
Requirements: Program provides support to Alabama residents for undergraduate non-sectarian secular education at non-profit Alabama colleges and universities not receiving direct appropriation from the state. Applications are available only at participating institutions.

Alabama Commission on Higher Education (Student Grants)
Amount: $2625.00 to $7500.00
Deadline: None
College Major: All Majors
Requirements: Grants are available to undergraduates, graduates and professional students who are US citizens or permanent residents. Amount of money awarded increased per school year. Contact a financial aid officer for more information.

Alabama Commission on Higher Education (Wallace-Folsom Prepaid College Tuition Program)
Amount: Varies
Deadline: None
College Major: All Majors
Requirements: Grants can be made available to Alabama resident college students who are sponsored in this program. Write for more information.

Alabama Scholarships for Dependents of Blind Parents
Amount: Variers
Deadline: None
College Major: All Majors
Requirements: Applicants must be residents of Alabama and from families in which one parent is blind. Students must attend a university or college in Alabama. Award covers tuition and expenses. For more information write to the above address.

Alaska

Alaska Commission on Post-Secondary Education (A W "Winn" Brindle Memorial Scholarship Loans)
State Office Building Pouch F
Juneau, AK 99801
Amount: Varies
Deadline: None
College Major: Fisheries/Fishery Sciences/Fishery Management/ Seafood Processing/Food Technology
Requirements: Scholarships are available to undergraduate and graduate full time college students who are majoring in the above fields. Applicants must be attending an accredited institution. Write for information.

Alaska Commission on Post-Secondary Education (Alaska Family Education Loans)
Amount: Up to $6500.00
Deadline: None
College Major: All Majors
Requirements: Loans are available to Alaska resident college students. Applicants must be full time students. Write for more application details.

Alaska Commission on Post-Secondary Education (Alaska Student Loans)
Amount: Up to $6500.00
Deadline: May 15
College Major: All Majors
Requirements: Loans are available to undergraduate and postgraduate Alaska state residents. Please write for more application details.

Alaska Commission on Post-Secondary Education (Alaska Teacher Loans)
Amount: Up to $1500.00
Deadline: May 31
College Major: Education
Requirements: Loans are available to Alaska high school seniors who have been admitted or are enrolled in an accredited teaching education program. Applicants must be full time students and be residents of Alaska for at least two years. Write for more information.

Alaska Commission on Post-Secondary Education (Half Time Student Loan Program)
Amount: $2000.00 to $2500.00
Deadline: May 15
College Major: All Majors
Requirements: Loans are available to Alaska residents who are part time students enrolled in an accredited college, university or vocational school in the state. Write for more information.

Alaska Commission on Post-Secondary Education (Michael Murphy Memorial Scholarship Loans)
Amount: Up to $1000.00
Deadline: April 1
College Major: Law Enforcement/Law/Probation and Parole/ Penology
Requirements: Scholarships are available to Alaska state resident undergraduates and graduates who are majoring in one of the above fields. Applicants must be full time students and be enrolled in an accredited institution. Write for more information.

Alaska Commission on Post-Secondary Education (Paul Douglas Scholarship Program)
Amount: $5000.00
Deadline: May 30
College Major: Education
Requirements: Scholarships are open to residents of Alaska who are planning to pursue a career in teaching. Applicant must be a graduating high school senior or a college undergraduate and a US citizen or legal resident. Scholarships must be repaid if recipients are not able to fulfill the obligation of teaching two years in a critical shortage area after graduation for every year of aid received. Please write for application and more information.

Alaska Commission on Post-Secondary Education (Robert C Thomas Memorial Scholarship)
Amount: Up to $1000.00
Deadline: Spring
College Major: Education/ Public Administration
Requirements: Scholarship loans are available to undergraduates and graduates majoring in one of the above fields of study. Applicants must be full time students and be enrolled in an accredited institution. Write for more information.

Alaska Commission on Post-Secondary Education (State Educational Incentive Grant Program)
Amount: $100.00 to $1500.00
Deadline: May 31
College Major: All Majors

Requirements: Grants are open to Alaska residents of at least two years who are accepted to or enrolled in an undergraduate program or similar certificate program. Applicant must show financial need. There are 120 grants per year. Write for more information.

American Samoa
American Samoa Government (Financial Aid Program)
Department of Education Office of Student Services
Pago Pago, American Samoa 96799
Amount: $5000.00
Deadline: April 30
College Major: All Majors
Requirements: These scholarships are available to American Samoa residents pursuing undergraduate or graduate study at any recognized academic institution. Students who are not from the islands are eligible if their parents are citizens of American Samoa. There are approximately 50 renewable awards given out per year. Write for more information.

Arizona
Arizona Commission for Post-Secondary Education (Paul Douglas Teacher Scholarship)
2020 North Central Avenue Suite 275
Phoenix, AZ 85004
Amount: $5000.00
Deadline: February 15
College Major: Education
Requirements: Scholarships are available to Arizona resident high school seniors who graduated in the upper 10% of their class. Applicants must be planning to study the above field. There are 20 awards given annually. Write for more information.

Arizona Commission for Post-Secondary Education (Student Incentive Grant Program)
Amount: Up to $2000.00
Deadline: June 30
College Major: All Majors
Requirements: Over 3000 awards are given to Arizona residents enrolled in participating Arizona colleges and universities. Both undergraduate and graduate students are suitable but some schools restrict grants to undergraduates or graduates. Applicants must be U.S. citizens or legal residents. Applications and information are available from a financial aid officer at each school.

Arkansas
Arkansas Department of Higher Education (Arkansas Academic Challenge)
114 East Capitol
Little Rock, AR 72201
Amount: $1000.00
Deadline: October 1
College Major: All Majors
Requirements: Funds are available each year to residents of Arkansas attending an undergraduate institution in Arkansas and pursuing an associate or bachelor's degree. Students must demonstrate financial need and satisfactory academic progress. Write for more information.

Arkansas Department of Higher Education (Emergency Secondary Education Loan)
Amount: Up to $2500.00
Deadline: April 1
College Major: Education

Requirements: Funds are available to Arkansas residents who are enrolled full-time in an undergraduate institution and are planning to pursue a degree in education. Recipients must teach for a minimum of two years in Arkansas following completion of studies or repay the total amount they received through the scholarship program. Students must teach secondary education in an area where there is a shortage of teachers and will receive 20% forgiveness on their loan for each year they teach. Write to the above address for more information.

Arkansas Department of Higher Education (Governor's Scholars)
Amount: $2000.00
Deadline: March 1
College Major: All Majors
Requirements: Grants are available each year to residents of Arkansas attending an accredited institution in Arkansas. Students must have a g.p.a. of at least 3.6, a 27 on the ACT or an SAT score of 1100. Write for more information.

Arkansas Department of Higher Education (Law Enforcement Officers Dependents Scholarship)
Amount: Tuition + Expenses
Deadline: Varies
College Major: All Majors
Requirements: Scholarships are available to dependents or spouses of Arkansas residents who were killed or totally disabled as a result of their law enforcement duties. Funds cover tuition and expenses at any accredited Arkansas state college or university. Write to the above address for more information.

Arkansas Department of Higher Education (MIA/KIA Dependents Scholarship)
Amount: Varies
Deadline: Varies
College Major: All Majors
Requirements: Scholarships are available to dependents or spouses of Arkansas residents who are MIA, KIA or POW. Funds cover tuition and expenses at any accredited Arkansas state college or university. Write to the above address for more information.

Arkansas Department of Higher Education (Paul Douglas Teacher Scholarship)
Amount: Up to $5000.00
Deadline: June 15
College Major: Education
Requirements: Funds are available to Arkansas residents who are enrolled full-time in an undergraduate institution and are planning to pursue a degree in education. Recipients must teach for a minimum of two years in Arkansas following completion of studies or repay the amount they received through the scholarship program. Write to the above address for more information.

Arkansas Department of Higher Education (Second Effort Scholarship)
Amount: $1000.00
Deadline: Varies
College Major: All Majors
Requirements: Funds are available each year to residents of Arkansas who scored in the top 10% on the GED exam in the year they are applying. Students must demonstrate satisfactory academic progress. Write for more information.

Arkansas Department of Higher Education (Student Assistance Grant Program)
Amount: $200.00 to $624.00
Deadline: July 1
College Major: All Majors

Requirements: Grants available each year to Arkansas residents studying at the undergraduate level at colleges or universities in Arkansas. Must show financial need and acceptable academic performance. Write for more information.

California

California Student Aid Commission (Assumption Program of Loans for Education)
PO Box 510845
Sacramento, CA 94245-0845
Amount: Up to $8000.00
Deadline: None
College Major: Teacher Education
Requirements: Loans are available to candidates for teaching credentials. Candidates must have completed the equivalent to at least 60 semester credits of undergraduate work and be presently registered in the equivalent of 10 credit hours. Applicants must also have taught either math, English, science, bilingual education, or special education for 3 years in a California public school. Write for more information.

California Student Aid Commission (Cal Grant 'A' Program)
Amount: $300.00 to $5250.00
Deadline: March 2
College Major: All Majors
Requirements: Applicants must be residents of California. These grants are open to low and middle income undergraduate students attending eligible schools in California. Selection is based on financial need and academic performance. Applicants must be U.S. citizens or legal residents. Approximately 1800 grants are given per year and they are renewable. Please write for application and more information.

California Student Aid Commission (Cal Grant 'B' Program)
Amount: $300.00 to $5250.00
Deadline: March 2
College Major: All Majors
Requirements: Applicants must be residents of California. These grants are open to low income undergraduate students attending two year and four year schools in California. Applicants must be U.S. citizens or legal residents. Please write for application and more information.

California Student Aid Commission (Cal Grant 'C' Program)
Amount: Up to $2360.00 (Tuition); up to $530.00 (Training Related costs)
Deadline: March 2
College Major: Vocational-Technical
Requirements: Applicant must be a U.S. citizen residing in California, or a legal resident. Grants are open to vocational and technical students attending a recognized vocational college in the state. Please write to the above address for information on the 1500 grants offered each year.

California Student Aid Commission (Child Development Teacher Loan Assumption Program)
Amount: Program Assumes Recipient's Debts
Deadline: None
College Major: Children's Instruction
Requirements: Funds are available to 100 college students who are pursuing a Children's Center Instructional or Supervision Permit. The program will assume all of the recipient's education loan debts. Write for more information.

California Student Aid Commission (Law Enforcement Personnel Dependents Grant Program)
Amount: Up to $1500.00

Deadline: None
College Major: All Majors
Requirements: These awards may be used for tuition, fees, books, supplies and living expenses and are open to California residents who are children of parents who have died or who were totally disabled while serving as California law enforcement officers. Applicants must demonstrate financial need. Write for more information

California Student Aid Commission (Paul Douglas Teacher Scholarship Program)
Amount: Up to $5000.00 per year up to four years
Deadline: Varies
College Major: Education
Requirements: Scholarships are available to California residents who are graduating high school seniors and undergraduate freshmen. Applicant must be a US citizen and be planning to strive for a career in teaching. Awards are to used at recognized college or university in California. Scholarship becomes a loan if obligation to teach for two years full time for each year funding is received is not fulfilled. Please write for application and more information.

California Student Aid Commission (Robert C. Byrd Honors Scholarship)
Amount: $1500.00
Deadline: Varies
College Major: All Majors
Requirements: Scholarships are available to high school graduates who have demonstrated outstanding academic achievement in high school and who show promise of continued academic achievement in college. These funds are only available for the first year of post-secondary study. Contact the above address for additional information.

Colorado

Colorado Commission on Higher Education (Colorado Student Incentive Grants-CSIG)
Colorado Heritage Center
1300 Broadway Second Floor
Boulder, CO 80203
Amount: Varies
Deadline: None
College Major: All Majors
Requirements: Undergraduate students attending an accredited college or university in Colorado are eligible. Awards are based on financial need. Contact a financial aid advisor, or write to the above address for more information.

Colorado Commission on Higher Education (Dependents Tuition Assistance Program)
Amount: Tuition
Deadline: None
College Major: All Majors
Requirements: Funds are available to dependents of state law enforcement officers, firemen or national guard members who were killed in the line of duty while serving in Colorado. Dependents of disabled veterans, MIA, or POW service personnel are also eligible. Write to the above address for more information.

Colorado Commission on Higher Education (Diversity Grants)
Amount: Varies
Deadline: None
College Major: All Majors

Requirements: Funds are available to all minority students enrolled in an accredited college or university in the state of Colorado. Contact a financial aid advisor, or the above address for more information.

Colorado Commission on Higher Education (Graduate Fellowships)
Amount: Varies
Deadline: None
College Major: All Majors
Requirements: Funds are available to graduate student attending an accredited college or university in the state of Colorado. Award amounts are based on academic merit. Contact a financial aid advisor or write to the above address for more information.

Colorado Commission on Higher Education (Graduate Grants)
Amount: Varies
Deadline: None
College Major: All Majors
Requirements: Grants are available to graduate students attending an accredited college or university in the state of Colorado. Award amounts are based on financial need. Contact a college advisor or write to the above address for more information.

Colorado Commission on Higher Education (Nursing Scholarship)
Amount: Varies
Deadline: April
College Major: Nursing
Requirements: Scholarships are available to Colorado residents pursuing a degree in nursing and who plan to practice in the state following completion of studies. Applications are available from the above address.

Colorado Commission on Higher Education (Part Time Grants)
Amount: Varies
Deadline: Varies
College Major: All Majors
Requirements: Grants are available to part time students attending an accredited Colorado college or university. Contact a financial aid advisor, or the above address for more information.

Colorado Commission on Higher Education (Paul Douglas Teacher Scholarship)
Amount: Varies
Deadline: None
College Major: Education
Requirements: Scholarships are awarded to high school seniors who are planning to pursue a degree in education. Write to the above address for more information.

Colorado Commission on Higher Education (Student Grants-CSG)
Amount: Varies
Deadline: None
College Major: All Majors
Requirements: Funds are available to undergraduate students attending an accredited college or university in Colorado. Award amounts are based on financial need. Contact a financial aid advisor, or write to the above address for more information.

Colorado Commission on Higher Education (Undergraduate Merit)
Amount: Varies
Deadline: None

College Major: All Majors

Requirements: Awards are given to undergraduate students currently enrolled full time in an accredited Colorado state college or university. Students who have demonstrated academic excellence and achievement are eligible. Write for more information or contact your college advisor.

Connecticut

Connecticut Department of Higher Education (Aid for Public College Students)
Office of Student Financial Aid
61 Woodland Street
Hartford, CT 06105
Amount: Varies
Deadline: None
College Major: All Majors
Requirements: Scholarships are available to Connecticut resident college students who are enrolled in a Connecticut public college or university. Write for more information.

Connecticut Department of Higher Education (Aid to Dependents of Deceased, Disabled, MIA Veterans)
Amount: $400.00
Deadline: None
College Major: All Majors
Requirements: Scholarships are open to Connecticut residents who are dependents of deceased (must be service related) or disabled war Veterans (total and permanent) or are MIA. Awards are for undergraduate study only. Write for more information.

Connecticut Department of Higher Education (Family Education Loan)
Amount: $2000.00 to $20000.00
Deadline: None
College Major: All Majors
Requirements: Loans are available to Connecticut resident college students who are registered no less than half time in a non profit university in Connecticut or elsewhere. Write for more information.

Connecticut Department of Higher Education (Independent College Student Grant)
Amount: Up to $6443.00
Deadline: None
College Major: All Majors
Requirements: Grants are available to Connecticut resident college students enrolled in an independent university or college in Connecticut. Write for more information.

Connecticut Department of Higher Education (Nursing Scholarship)
Amount: Varies
Deadline: Varies
College Major: Nursing
Requirements: Applicants must be a Connecticut resident enrolled full-time in a three-year hospital school of nursing program in Connecticut or in a two- or four-year nursing program at a Connecticut college. Awards will be given based on academic standing and financial need. Write for more information.

Connecticut Department of Higher Education (Robert C. Byrd Honors Scholarship)
Amount: $1500.00
Deadline: Varies
College Major: All Majors

Requirements: This award is available to Connecticut high school seniors in the top 3 percent of their class. Judging criteria consists of SAT scores and high school ranking. Write or call for more information.

Connecticut Department of Higher Education (Scholastic Achievement Grant)
Amount: Up to $2000.00
Deadline: February 15
College Major: All Majors
Requirements: Grants are available to graduating seniors who are residents of Connecticut. Applicants must be US citizens and meet at least one of the following requirements: be in the upper 20% of their class, have a minimum SAT score of 1100, or a minimum ACT score of 27. Write for more details.

Connecticut Department of Higher Education (State Scholastic Grant Program)
Amount: $300.00 to $2000.00
Deadline: January 15
College Major: All Majors
Requirements: This grant is available to Connecticut high school seniors and graduates who ranked in the top 33% of their class or scored 1100 or above on the SAT exam. This scholarship applies to undergraduate study at a university or college in the New England area. Applicant must be a US citizen. There are 3000 awards available. Please contact in writing for further information.

Connecticut Department of Higher Education (Tuition Aid for Needy Students)
Amount: Varies
Deadline: None
College Major: All Majors
Requirements: Scholarships are available to college students attending a Connecticut public university. Write for more information.

Connecticut Department of Higher Education (Tuition Aid Waiver for Veterans)
Amount: Tuition
Deadline: None
College Major: All Majors
Requirements: Scholarships are available to Connecticut resident veterans who are enrolled in a Connecticut college and were Connecticut residents at the time of entry into service. Children of Vietnam veterans who are POWs or MIAs are also eligible. Write for more information.

Connecticut Department of Higher Education (Tuition Waiver for Senior Citizens)
Amount: Tuition
Deadline: None
College Major: All Majors
Requirements: Scholarships are available to senior citizen Connecticut residents who are 62 years old or older and are enrolled in a Connecticut public university or college. Write for more information.

Connecticut Department of Higher Education (Teacher Incentive Loan Program Academic Loan Program)
Amount: $3000.00 to $5000.00
Deadline: None
College Major: Education
Requirements: Scholarships are available to undergraduate students attending an accredited college or university in Connecticut. Applicant must be planning to teach in an assigned shortage area in Connecticut and be a US citizen or legal resident. Selection is based on scholastic excellence and financial need. Please write for application and more information.

Delaware

Delaware Higher Education Commission (B Bradford Barnes Scholarship)
Carvel State Office Building
820 North French Street
Wilmington, DE 19801
Amount: Varies
Deadline: February 5
College Major: All Majors
Requirements: Applicants must be Delaware high school seniors who have accepted admission from the University of Delaware. Write for more information.

Delaware Higher Education Commission (Benefits for Children of Deceased Veterans and Others)
Amount: Varies
Deadline: None
College Major: All Majors
Requirements: Applicants must be residents of Delaware and the children of deceased State Police Officers or military veterans whose cause of death was duty related. Benefits are awarded to students who attend a Delaware public college. Write for complete information.

Delaware Higher Education Commission (Christa McAuliffe Teacher Scholarship Loan)
Amount: $1000.00
Deadline: March 31
College Major: Education
Requirements: Applicants must be Delaware residents who pursue teaching careers and plan to teach at Delaware public schools. Write for more information.

Delaware Higher Education Commission (Delaware Nursing Scholarship Loan)
Amount: Up to $3000.00
Deadline: March 31
College Major: Nursing
Requirements: Applicants must be Delaware residents pursuing an education as a Registered or Practical Nurse. Write for complete information.

Delaware Higher Education Commission (Delaware Optometric Institutional Aid)
Amount: $4000.00
Deadline: None
College Major: Optometry
Requirements: Applicants must be residents of Delaware pursuing an education in Optometry. Write for complete details.

Delaware Higher Education Commission (Delaware Post-secondary Scholarship Fund)
Amount: $200.00 to $1000.00
Deadline: April 15
College Major: All Majors
Requirements: These funds are available to full time undergraduate students who have been Delaware residents for at least one year. Awards can be used at recognized institution for higher education. Applicants must be U.S. citizens or legal residents to apply. Write for application and more information.

Delaware Higher Education Commission (Diamond State Scholarship)
Amount: $1000.00
Deadline: March 31

College Major: All Majors
Requirements: Applicants must be Delaware high school seniors. There are approximately 50 renewable awards per year. Write for more information.

Delaware Higher Education Commission (Governor's Workforce Development Grant)
Amount: Varies
Deadline: None
College Major: All Majors
Requirements: Financial assistance is provided for part-time students employed by a small business. Applicants must meet income requirements. Write for more details.

Delaware Higher Education Commission (Paul Douglas Teacher Scholarship Loan)
Amount: Up to $5000.00
Deadline: March 31
College Major: Education
Requirements: Applicants must be Delaware residents who pursue teaching careers and plan to teach at Delaware schools. Write for more information.

Delaware Higher Education Commission (Robert C Byrd Scholarship)
Amount: $1500.00
Deadline: March 31
College Major: All Majors
Requirements: Applicants must be Delaware high school seniors. There are approximately 12 awards per year available to students who display extended excellence. Write for more information.

District of Columbia

District of Columbia Office of Post-secondary Education (Paul Douglas Teacher Scholarship)
2100 Martin Luther King Jr. Avenue SE, Suite 401
Washington, DC 20020
Amount: $5000.00
Deadline: Varies
College Major: Education
Requirements: Scholarships are open to Washington DC residents of at least one year. Recipients must agree to teach for at least two years for every year assistance was received. Please write for application and more information.

District of Columbia Office of Post-secondary Education, Research and Assistance (TERI Supplemental Loan)
Amount: $2000.00 to $20000.00
Deadline: None
College Major: All Majors
Requirements: Scholarships are available to graduate and undergraduate students who are attending a university or college in the US. Write for more information.

District of Columbia Office of Post-secondary Education (Supplemental Educational Opportunity Grant)
Amount: $100.00 to $4000.00
Deadline: January 1
College Major: All Majors
Requirements: Grants are open to undergraduate students enrolled at least half time. Applicant must be a permanent resident or US citizen. Please write for application and information.

District of Columbia Office Post-secondary Education, Research and Assistance (District of Columbia Nurses Training Corps Program)
Amount: Up to $22000.00
Deadline: June 1
College Major: Nursing
Requirements: Funds are available to District of Columbia resident nursing students who are studying nursing at one of the following institutions: University of DC, Catholic University of America, Howard University, Georgetown University, Margaret Murray Washington Career Development Center. Must work two years for the District of Columbia for every year of scholarship funds received. Write for more information.

Florida

Florida Department of Education (Challenger Astronauts Memorial Scholarship Program)
Office of Student Financial Assistance
1344 Florida Educational Center
Tallahassee, FL 32399
Amount: $4000.00 per year
Deadline: April 1
College Major: Liberal Arts/Education
Requirements: Applicant must be a Florida resident for at least one year in order to apply to this program. Applicants must also be Florida Public High School seniors enrolling in an institution of higher learning for the first time. Students must attend a state university or community college in Florida, seeking a career in liberal arts or teaching. Each school may select one nominee to compete for the awards. Write for complete details.

Florida Department of Education ('Chappie' James Most Promising Teacher Scholarship Loan Program)
Amount: $4000.00
Deadline: March 1
College Major: All Majors
Requirements: Outstanding high school seniors who intend to pursue a career in teaching in Florida are eligible to apply. Applicant must be in the top 25% of their senior class, and have at least a 2.5 g.p.a.. Applicant must submit a list of extracurricular activities, letters of recommendation and an essay on the applicant's interest on teaching. The loan recipient must attend full time at an eligible Florida institution. The loan is repaid by teaching in Florida after graduation or paying cash. Please write at the address above for complete information.

Florida Department of Education (College Career Work Experience Program)
Amount: Varies
Deadline: None
College Major: All Majors
Requirements: Residents of Florida of at least two years are eligible. This program is open to undergraduate students who are in need of financial aid, attending at least half time at a Florida institution. This program provides students with off-campus employment in jobs related to their declared major area of study or career interest. Please write to the given address for complete information.

Florida Department of Education (Confederate Memorial Scholarships)
Amount: $150.00 per year
Deadline: March 1
College Major: All Majors
Requirements: Residents of Florida and who are descendants of a Confederate soldier or sailor are eligible to apply. Applicant must be attending a public college or university in Florida as a full time student. Please contact the address given above for application and complete information.

Florida Department of Education (Critical Teacher Shortage Loan Forgiveness Program)
Amount: Up to $10000.00
Deadline: July 15
College Major: Education
Requirements: This program is open to certified public school teachers in Florida teaching for the first time in a critical teacher shortage area. The program provides for repayment of education loans in return for teaching in the Department of Education designated critical shortage area public schools in Florida. Applicants must apply during the first 12 months they are certified and teaching full time in the shortage area. Please write for application an more information.

Florida Department of Education (Florida Graduate Scholars Fund)
Amount: $10000.00
Deadline: April 1
College Major: Engineering
Requirements: Awards are made on a first come, first serve basis. Applicant must have been a recipient of the Florida Undergraduate Scholars Fund or have a 3.5 g.p.a. during the last two years of college and have a minimum combined GRE score of 1200. All applicants must enroll on a full time basis as first time graduate students at a Florida post secondary institution as identified by Section 240.4025, Florida Statutes. Renewal applicants and Florida residents have the highest priority. Write for further information.

Florida Department of Education (Florida Student Assistance Grants)
Amount: $200.00 to $1500.00
Deadline: May 15
College Major: All Majors
Requirements: Grants are available to U.S. citizens or legal residents and residents of Florida for at least two years. Applicants must be full-time undergraduate students at eligible institutions in Florida and be in need of financial aid. Please write at the address given above for complete information.

Florida Department of Education (Florida Students Regents Scholarship)
Amount: $5000.00
Deadline: None
College Major: All Majors
Requirements: This scholarship is awarded to students who were or are student members of the Florida Board of Regents. Please write to the address given above for complete information.

Florida Department of Education (Florida Tuition Voucher Grants)
Amount: $1150.00 to $2000.00
Deadline: None
College Major: All Majors
Requirements: U.S. citizens or legal residents who are residents of Florida of at least two years. Applicant must be a full time undergraduate student attending a recognized college or university in Florida. Awards are not need based. Please contact the address above for complete information.

Florida Department of Education (Florida Undergraduate Scholars' Fund)
Amount: $2500.00 to $4000.00
Deadline: April 1
College Major: All Majors
Requirements: Scholarships are open to US citizens or legal residents and have been Florida residents for at least two years. Applicant must have been a finalist in the National Merit Scholarship, have a 3.5 g.p.a., and have at least a 1200 score on the SAT or a score of 29 on the ACT. Applicant must also enroll in a Florida public or private school. Please write at the address given above for complete information.

Florida Department of Education (Florida Vocational Gold Seal Endorsement Scholarship Program)
Amount: $2000.00
Deadline: April 1
College Major: Vocational/Technical Study
Requirements: Scholarships are available to Florida residents who are high school graduates and plan to attend a vocational or technical school. Applicants must have a Florida Gold Seal Endorsement. Write for more information.

Florida Department of Education (Jose Marti Scholarship Challenge Grant Fund)
Amount: $2000.00 per year
Deadline: May 15
College Major: All Majors
Requirements: Hispanic Americans who are US citizens or legal residents and have been residents of Florida for at least two years are eligible to apply. Applicants must be enrolled as full time undergraduate or graduate students at eligible Florida institutions and have at least a 3.0 g.p.a.. This is a need based award. Please contact the above address for complete information.

Florida Department of Education (Mary McLeod Bethune Scholarship Challenge Grant)
Amount: $3000.00
Deadline: April 30
College Major: All Majors
Requirements: Grants are available to high school seniors who are Florida residents for at least one year and are enrolled in either Florida Agricultural and Mechanical University, Bethune-Cookman College, Edward Waters College, or Florida Memorial College. Applicants be registered for at least 12 credits, have a g.p.a. of at least 3.0 and have participated in the college level communication and computation testing (CLAST) program. Write for more information.

Florida Department of Education (National Science Scholars Program)
Amount: Up to $5000.00
Deadline: Varies
College Major: Computer Science/Engineering/Math/Related Fields
Requirements: Scholarships are available to high school graduates who commit to majoring in one of the above areas. Applicants must have a strong academic record and good test scores. Write to the above address for more information.

Florida Department of Education (Nicaraguan and Haitian Scholarship Program)
Amount: $4000.00 to 45000.00
Deadline: Varies
College Major: All Majors
Requirements: Funds are available to Nicaraguan and Haitian students who are Florida residents and are planning on attending an accredited college or university in Florida. Applicants must have a g.p.a. of 3.0 or higher. Write to the above address for more information.

Florida Department of Education (Paul Douglas Teacher Scholarship)
Amount: $5000.00 to $20000.00
Deadline: April 15
College Major: Education
Requirements: Scholarships are available to Florida resident high school graduates and college students who are majoring in the above field. Applicants must US citizens, have a g.p.a. of 3.0, place in the upper

10% of their high school, and score at or above the 40 percentile on the SAT or ACT tests. Applicants must be or plan to be full time students. Write for more information.

Florida Department of Education (Robert C. Byrd Honors Scholarships)
Amount: $1500.00
Deadline: None
College Major: All Majors
Requirements: Scholarships are available to high school seniors who are residents of Florida and are planning to attend a non profit college or university. Applicants must have a g.p.a. of at least 3.85 and a SAT or ACT score at or above the 75 percentile. Must be a US citizen. Write for information.

Florida Department of Education (Scholarships for Children of Deceased or Disabled Veterans)
Amount: Tuition and fees
Deadline: April 1
College Major: All Majors
Requirements: Children or spouses of deceased or 100% disabled qualified war veterans, POWs and MIAs are eligible to apply. Applicant must be Florida resident of a minimum of five year, a US citizen and attending a public college or university in Florida. Scholarships are renewable. Write for application and complete details.

Florida Department of Education (Seminole/Miccosukee Indian Scholarships)
Amount: Varies
Deadline: None specified
College Major: All Majors
Requirements: Members of Seminole or Miccosukee Indian Tribes who are US citizens, Florida residents, and enrolled as full or part time undergraduate or graduate students at a Florida institution are eligible to apply. Scholarships are renewable. Please write to the above address for complete information.

Florida Department of Education (Teacher Scholarship Loan Program)
Amount: $1500.00 to $8000.00
Deadline: March 1
College Major: Education
Requirements: Scholarships awarded to full-time undergraduate juniors or seniors enrolled in a state authorized teacher education program in a Florida institution for higher learning. Recipients are obligated to teach in a Florida critical shortage areas or the scholarship becomes a loan. There are 376 awards per year. Write for complete details.

Florida Department of Education (Virgil Hawkins Fellows Scholarship)
Amount: $5000.00
Deadline: Varies
College Major: Law
Requirements: Funds are available to first year minority law students who are enrolled in an accredited college or university in Florida. Applicants must have recommendation from the Dean of the law school. For more information write to the above address.

Georgia
Georgia Student Finance Authority (Charles McDaniel Teacher Scholarship Fund)
2082 East Exchange Place, Suite 200
Tucker, GA 30084
Amount: Varies
Deadline: Varies
College Major: Education

Requirements: Scholarships are open to undergraduate upperclassmen who are Georgia resident of at least one year. Applicant must have a minimum g.p.a. of 3.25 (4.0 scale), US citizen or legal resident and committed to pursuing a career as teacher at the elementary and secondary level. Please write for application and more information.

Georgia Student Finance Authority (Congressional Teacher Scholarship Program)
Amount: $5000.00 per year up to four years
Deadline: May 1
College Major: Education
Requirements: This program is open to high school seniors who live in Georgia (at least 12 months) and plan to study at the undergraduate level in Georgia. This is program is designed to help outstanding students to strive for career in teaching at pre-school, elementary and secondary levels. Applicant must be a US citizen or legal resident. Recipients are obligated to teach for two years for each year of aid received or half that for teaching in a critical teacher shortage area. Please write for complete details.

Georgia Student Finance Authority (Direct Student Scholarship Loan Program)
Amount: $1400.00 Undergraduates; $1800.00 Graduates
Deadline: July 1
College Major: All Majors
Requirements: Georgia residents are eligible to apply to this program. Applicant must be planning to pursue studies in the fields where there is a shortage of personnel in Georgia. Awards need not to be repaid if they work in Georgia for one year for every year funding was received. Please write for application and more information.

Georgia Student Finance Authority (Governor's Scholarship Program)
Amount: $1350.00 per year
Deadline: Varies
College Major: All Majors
Requirements: Full time freshmen at an eligible Georgia university or college who have been Georgia residents for at least 12 months, and are designated Georgia scholars, can apply for these scholarships which are renewable up to three years. Applicants must enter college within seven months of their high school graduation and they must be U.S. citizens or legal residents. Write for more information.

Georgia Student Finance Authority (Law Enforcement Personnel Dependents Grant)
Amount: $2000.00
Deadline: August 1
College Major: All Majors
Requirements: Georgia residents accepted in colleges or universities in Georgia who are children of Georgia law enforcement officers or firemen or prison guards killed or permanently disabled in the line of duty are eligible to apply. Applicants must be US citizens or legal residents. The grants are renewable up to $8000.00 over four years time. Write for more information.

Georgia Student Finance Authority (Private College Tuition Equalization Grant)
Amount: $825.00
Deadline: September
College Major: All Majors
Requirements: Grants are available to students who are attending a private college or university in Georgia. Applicant must have been a resident of Georgia of at least one year and a US citizen or legal resident. Please write for application and more information.

Georgia Student Finance Authority (Student Incentive Grant)
Amount: $150.00 to $450.00

Deadline: June 1
College Major: All Majors
Requirements: Resident of Georgia of at least one year are eligible to apply. Applicant must be attending a college, university or vocational-technical, in need of financial aid and a US citizen or legal resident. Please write for application and more information.

Hawaii

Hawaii Post Secondary Education Commission (Hawaii Student Incentive Grants)
Financial Aids Office
2442 Campus Road
Honolulu, HI 96822-2292
Amount: Varies
Deadline: None
College Major: All Majors
Requirements: Applicants must demonstrate financial need and be attending school full-time. This grant is available to Hawaii residents. Write for more information.

Hawaii Post Secondary Education Commission (Health Professions Loans)
Amount: Varies
Deadline: None
College Major: Medicine
Requirements: Applicants must demonstrate financial need and be attending the School of Medicine full-time. Write for more information.

Hawaii Post Secondary Education Commission (Members of the National Guard and Reserve Units)
Amount: Varies
Deadline: Varies
College Major: All Majors
Requirements: Scholarships are open to residents of Hawaii who are members of the National Guard or the Army Reserves. Please write for application and more information.

Hawaii Post Secondary Education Commission (Nursing Student Loans)
Amount: Varies
Deadline: None
College Major: Nursing
Requirements: Applicants must demonstrate financial need and be enrolled at least part-time in nursing programs. Write for more information.

Hawaii Post Secondary Education Commission (Presidential Achievement Scholarships)
Amount: $4000.00
Deadline: Varies
College Major: All Majors
Requirements: Scholarships are open to residents of Hawaii who are undergraduate juniors enrolled at Manoa, Hilo or West Oahu campuses of the University of Hawaii. Please write for application and more information.

Hawaii Post Secondary Education Commission (Regents Scholarship for Academic Excellence)
Amount: $4000.00
Deadline: None
College Major: All Majors
Requirements: Applicants must be Hawaii residents and incoming freshmen. The scholarship is renewable for qualified students. Write for complete details.

Hawaii Post Secondary Education Commission (State Higher Education Loans)
Amount: Varies
Deadline: None
College Major: All Majors
Requirements: Applicants must demonstrate financial need and be attending school full-time. This loan is available to undergraduate and graduate Hawaii residents. Write for more information.

Hawaii Post Secondary Education Commission (Tuition Waivers)
Amount: Varies
Deadline: None
College Major: All Majors
Requirements: Applicants must demonstrate financial need or achievement/service to the University. Write for complete details.

Hawaii Post Secondary Education Commission (Veterans or Dependent of Deceased Veterans Scholarship)
Amount: Varies
Deadline: Varies
College Major: All Majors
Requirements: Scholarships are open to Vietnam Veterans or their dependents who are residents of Hawaii and are undergraduate students. Please write for application and more information.

Idaho

Idaho Board of Education (Paul L. Fowler Memorial Scholarship Program)
Len B. Jordan Building, Room 307
650 West State Street
Boise, ID 83720
Amount: $2380.00
Deadline: January 31
College Major: All Majors
Requirements: Scholarships are available to Idaho resident high school seniors who are enrolled as full time college students. Applicants must take the ACT test. Write for more information.

Idaho Board of Education (Scholarship Program)
Amount: $2650.00
Deadline: January 31
College Major: All Majors
Requirements: Scholarships are available to Idaho resident high school seniors who are enrolled as full time college students. Applicants must take the ACT test. Write for more information.

Idaho State Board of Education (Paul Douglas Teacher Scholarship)
Amount: $5000.00
Deadline: February 15
College Major: Education
Requirements: Candidates must be pursuing a teaching degree full time at an Idaho college or university, must rank in the top tenth of their graduating class, and commit to teaching for two years for each year of scholarship award. Approximately 15 renewable scholarships are awarded annually. Contact the Scholarship Assistant for further information.

Illinois

Illinois Student Assistance Commission (Bonus Incentive Grant)
1755 Lake Cook Road

Deerfield, IL 60015
Amount: Varies
Deadline: None
College Major: All Majors
Requirements: Grants are available to Illinois college students who have Illinois College Savings Bonds. Applicants may attend an Illinois two or four year university or college. Write for more information.

Illinois Student Assistance Commission (Correctional Officer's Grant)
Amount: Up to $3500.00
Deadline: Varies
College Major: All Majors
Requirements: Funds for this grant pay for the tuition and fees that are mandatory for the spouse or children of an Illinois Correctional Officer killed or at least 90 percent disabled in the line of duty. Recipients must be attending an approved Illinois public or private two or four-year college, university or hospital school at least half-time. Please write for more information.

Illinois Student Assistance Commission (Illinois National Guard Grant)
Amount: Varies
Deadline: Varies
College Major: All Majors
Requirements: Applicants must be company grade officers and enlistees up to the captain rank. These people must have served one year of active duty or are on active duty currently. Tuition and a variety of fees are paid by this grant for eight semesters or 12 quarters of either graduate study or undergraduate study at a public, two or four-year, university or college. See the school Financial Aid Administrator if you have any questions.

Illinois Student Assistance Commission (Illinois Veteran Grant)
Amount: varies
Deadline: Varies
College Major: All Majors
Requirements: This grant pays for tuition and fees that are approved to qualified veterans with at least one year of active duty in the U.S. Armed Forces. You are eligible if you are in graduate or undergraduate study at a public two- or four-year university or college in Illinois. Veterans must be a resident of Illinois at the time of entering the service as well as a resident within six months of departing from the service. Write for more information.

Illinois Student Assistance Commission (Merit Recognition Scholarship)
Amount: $1000.00
Deadline: Varies
College Major: All Majors
Requirements: Funds are available to high school seniors in the top 5% of their class who are enrolling in an accredited college, university or vocational school in the state of Illinois. Write to the above address for more information.

Illinois Student Assistance Commission (Minority Teachers of Illinois)
Amount: $5000.00 per year
Deadline: Varies
College Major: Education
Requirements: Funds are available yearly to minority full time undergraduate students who are pursuing a degree in education. Recipients of the award must agree to work one year for each year they receive financial assistance, in an area which has 30% or more minority students. If recipients do not fulfill these requirements, the award becomes a loan to be paid back. Write to the above address for more information.

Illinois Student Assistance Commission (Monetary Award Program)
Amount: Up to $3500.00
Deadline: Varies
College Major: All Majors
Requirements: A maximum award is determined each year which covers tuition as well as mandatory fees. This grant is based on financial need. Applicants must be studying at a public or private, two or four year, college, university, or medical school at least as a half-time student. Please write for more information.

Illinois Student Assistance Commission (Paul Douglas Teacher Scholarship)
Amount: Up to $5000.00
Deadline: August 1 (freshmen); June 1 (other)
College Major: Education
Requirements: Undergraduate students who are residents of Illinois and US citizens or legal residents are eligible for these funds if they rank in the top tenth of their high school class and are planning to attend an approved Illinois school full time in a qualified Teacher Education Program. Recipients must agree to teach two years for each year of the scholarship or repay the money with interest. The awards are renewable. Write to the above address for more information.

Illinois Student Assistance Commission (Police Officer/Fire Officer Grant)
Amount: Up to $3500.00
Deadline: Varies
College Major: All Majors
Requirements: This grant goes to the spouse and children (under the age of 25) of Illinois Fire/Police Officers killed while on duty. Mandatory tuition and fees are paid to attend an approved public or private two- or four-year university, college or hospital school at least half-time. If you have any questions please contact your financial aid administrator at your school.

Illinois Student Assistance Commission (Student-to-Student Grant)
Amount: Varies
Deadline: Varies
College Major: All Majors
Requirements: This grant is based on financial need. The contributions come from students and the amount is matched by this commission. You are eligible if you are attending a participating public two or four-year university or college in Illinois. If you have any questions please call or write your financial aid administrator at your university.

Indiana

Indiana State Student Assistance Commission (Higher Education Award, Freedom Choice Grants)
Ista Center Building
150 West Market Street, Suite 500
Indianapolis, IN 46204
Amount: $200.00 to $3700.00
Deadline: March 1
College Major: All Majors
Requirements: Scholarships are open to Indiana residents who are accepted to or enrolled in eligible Indiana institutions as full time undergraduate students. Applicant must be a US citizen or legal resident. There are 36,000 grants per year. Write for more information.

Indiana State Student Assistance Commission (Indiana Minority Teacher & Special Education Scholarships)
Amount: $1000.00 to $4000.00
Deadline: May 1

College Major: Education
Requirements: Scholarships are available to African-American or Hispanic Indiana resident college students planning a career in the above field of study. Must be a full time undergraduate or graduate, and have a g.p.a. of 2.0 or more. Write for more information.

Indiana State Student Assistance Commission (Indiana Nursing Scholarships)
Amount: $100.00 to $5000.00
Deadline: July 1
College Major: Nursing
Requirements: Scholarships are available to Indiana resident nursing students who will agree in writing to work in the state for two years after graduation. Must have a g.p.a. of at least 2.0. Write for information.

Indiana State Student Assistance Commission (Lilly Endowment Educational Scholarships)
Amount: $200.00 to $1400.00
Deadline: March 1
College Major: All Majors
Requirements: Students pursuing their 1st degree who are Indiana residents are eligible for these awards. Must attend an Indiana academic institution. Applicant must be a US citizen. There are 17,000 awards each year which are renewable. Write for more information.

Indiana State Students Assistance Commission (Paul Douglas Teacher Scholarship)
Amount: $5000.00
Deadline: March 1
College Major: Education
Requirements: There are approximately 20 scholarships available each year for Indiana residents who can demonstrate financial need and are willing to submit an essay and a resume. Applicants must have a minimum 3.0 g.p.a. and proof of full time enrollment to apply for award renewal. Write for more information.

Indiana State Students Assistance Commission (Special Education Services Scholarship)
Amount: Varies
Deadline: March 1
College Major: Special Education
Requirements: Funds are available to Indiana residents accepted to or currently attending an Indiana institution full time who plan to pursue a course of study to enable them to teach special education or occupational and physical therapy in the state.

Iowa

Iowa College Student Aid Commission (Iowa Grants)
201 Jewett Building
914 Grand Avenue
Des Moines, IA 50309-2824
Amount: Up to $1000.00
Deadline: Varies
College Major: All Majors
Requirements: Applicants must be residents of Iowa and United States citizens, on a permanent visa or a refugee. Grants are available to currently enrolled students or students planning to enroll part time in an eligible Iowa school.

Iowa College Student Aid Commission (Iowa Vocational-Technical Tuition Grants)
Amount: $600.00
Deadline: April 20

College Major: All Majors
Requirements: Applicants must be residents of Iowa and United States citizens, on a permanent visa or a refugee. Grants are available to currently enrolled students or students planning to enroll full time in a career option or career education course at an Iowa community college.

Iowa College Student Aid Commission (State of Iowa Scholarships)
Amount: $100.00 to $500.00 per year
Deadline: November 1
College Major: All Majors
Requirements: Applicants must be high school seniors and be ranked in the upper 15% of their class. Scholarships are available to residents of the state of Iowa.

Iowa College Student Aid Commission (Iowa Tuition Grants)
Amount: Up to $2650.00
Deadline: April 20
College Major: All Majors
Requirements: Applicants must be residents of Iowa and United States citizens. Non-residents must be on a permanent visa or qualify for refugee status. Grants are available to currently enrolled students or students planning to enroll at least part-time.

Kansas

Kansas Board of Regents (Kansas Tuition Grant)
400 Southwest Eighth
Capitol Tower, Suite 609
Topeka, KS 66603
Amount: $200.00 to $1700.00
Deadline: March 15
College Major: All Majors
Requirements: Kansas residents enrolled full time in undergraduate study at independent or private institutions in Kansas may apply. Applicants must be U.S. citizens and maintain at least a 2.0 cumulative g.p.a. There are 3600 renewable grants disbursed each year. Write for more information.

Kansas Board of Regents (Minority Scholarship)
Amount: Up to $1500.00
Deadline: March 5
College Major: All Majors
Requirements: Scholarships are open to minority students who are attending schools in Kansas. Applicant must demonstrate outstanding academic achievement. Please write for application and more information.

Kansas Board of Regents (Nursing Scholarship)
Amount: $2500.00 to $3500.00
Deadline: May 1
College Major: Nursing
Requirements: Scholarships are open to students pursuing nursing and are planning to practice nursing in Kansas. Please write for application and more information.

Kansas Board of Regents (Paul T. Douglas Teacher Scholarship)
Amount: $5000.00 per year
Deadline: March 1
College Major: Education

Requirements: Scholarships are open to students pursuing a teaching certificate and are planning to teach in Kansas after graduation. Applicant must demonstrate high academic achievement. Please write for application and more information.

Kansas Board of Regents (State Scholarships Program)
Amount: $50.00 to $1000.00
Deadline: April 21
College Major: All Majors
Requirements: Kansas residents who graduated from Kansas high schools and are currently studying at an eligible college or technical-vocational college in Kansas may apply for these scholarships. Applicants must maintain a minimum a 3.0 g.p.a.. There are 1200 renewable scholarships given each year. Write for more information.

Kansas Board of Regents (Vocational Educational Scholarship)
Amount: Up to $1500.00
Deadline: Varies
College Major: All Majors
Requirements: Scholarships are open to students planning to enroll or attend a vocational-technical school in Kansas. Please write for application and more information.

Kansas Commission on Veterans' Affairs (Scholarships)
Amount: Payment of fees only
Deadline: Prior to enrollment
College Major: All Majors
Requirements: Scholarships are offered to children of military personnel who entered service in the US Armed Forces while a resident of Kansas and now qualify as a POW, MIA, or KIA. Scholarships are renewable. Write for more information.

Kentucky
Kentucky Higher Education Assistance Authority (College Access Program Grant)
1050 US 127 South, Suite 102
Frankfort, KY 40601-4323
Amount: Varies
Deadline: Open
College Major: All Majors
Requirements: This program is open to undergraduate students enrolled in an accredited college or university. Applicant must be a permanent resident or US citizen and must not be in default on any grants or loans. Please write for application and more information.

Kentucky Higher Education Assistance Authority (Kentucky Tuition Grant)
Amount: $50.00 to $1200.00
Deadline: Open
College Major: All Majors
Requirements: Grants are available to full time undergraduate students who are Kentucky residents enrolled in an accredited college or university. Applicant must be a permanent resident or US citizen, not be in default in any grants or loans and demonstrate financial need. Recipients must show satisfactory academic progress. Please write for application and more information.

Kentucky Higher Education Assistance Authority (Paul Douglas Teacher Scholarship)
Amount: $5000.00 per year
Deadline: April 15
College Major: All Majors

Requirements: Scholarships are open to full time undergraduate students pursuing a teacher's certificate who are Kentucky residents. Applicant must have graduated in the top 10% of their class, and a permanent resident or U.S. citizen. Recipients are obligated to teach for two years in school where there is a teacher shortage. Please write for application and more information.

Kentucky Higher Education Assistance Authority (Student Loan Program)
Amount: $2500.00 to $15000
Deadline: None specified
College Major: All Majors
Requirements: Residents of Kentucky who are registered or admitted for enrollment at least half time at a recognized academic institution are eligible to apply. Applicants must be U.S. citizens or legal residents. Please write for more information.

Kentucky Higher Education Assistance Authority (Teacher Scholarship)
Amount: $2500.00
Deadline: April 15
College Major: All Majors
Requirements: Scholarships are open to full time students pursuing a teacher's certificate who are residents of Kentucky. Applicant must be ranked in the top 10% of their class, have at least a 2.5 g.p.a., and not be in default in any grants or loans. Please write for application and more information.

Louisiana
Louisiana Office of Student Financial Assistance (Honors Scholarship Program)
P.O. Box 91202
Baton Rouge, LA 70821
Amount: Tuition & Expenses
Deadline: Varies
College Major: All Majors
Requirements: Scholarships are open to Louisiana residents who are U.S. citizens and are enrolled or planning to enroll in a college or university in Louisiana. This program covers the cost of tuition and expenses. Applicants must be full time undergraduate students.

Louisiana Office of Student Financial Assistance (Paul Douglas Teacher Scholarship)
Amount: $5000.00 to $20000.00
Deadline: April 15
College Major: All Majors
Requirements: Scholarships are open to Louisiana residents who are U.S. citizens and who promise to teach two years anywhere in the US for each year of funding or repay the scholarship. Applicants must have graduated in the top tenth of their class with a minimum 3.0 g.p.a., and have a minimum ACT score of 22, a minimum ENACT score of 23, or a minimum SAT score of 920. Contact the Scholarship Grant Director for further information.

Louisiana Office of Student Financial Assistance (Rockefeller Wildlife Scholarship)
Amount: $1000.00 per year
Deadline: April 1
College Major: Forestry/Marine Sciences/Wildlife
Requirements: Funds are available to Louisiana residents who are U.S. citizens and are enrolled or planning to enroll in a college, university or vocational school in Louisiana. Applicants must be full time undergraduates majoring in the above areas. Students must fill out the Application for Federal Student Aid to be considered. Write to the above address for further information.

Louisiana Office of Student Financial Assistance (Special Scholarships)
Amount: Tuition & Expenses
Deadline: Varies
College Major: All Majors
Requirements: Funds are available to Louisiana residents whose parents where law enforcement officers, firefighters, sanitation workers, school teachers or correction officers who were killed or permanently disabled as a result of their occupation. Applicants must be U.S. citizens and enrolled or planning to enroll in a college or university and demonstrate financial need. Funds cover tuition, room and board and $125.00 cash grant for four years of study. Write to the above address for further information.

Louisiana Office of Student Financial Assistance (State Student Incentive Grant)
Amount: $200.00 to $2000.00
Deadline: Varies
College Major: All Majors
Requirements: Grants are open to Louisiana residents who are U.S. citizens and are enrolled or planning to enroll in a college, university or vocational school in Louisiana. Applicants must be full time undergraduate students and demonstrate financial need. Write to the above address for more information.

Louisiana Office of Student Financial Assistance (T.H. Harris State Academic Scholarship)
Amount: $400.00 per year
Deadline: April 1
College Major: All Majors
Requirements: Funds are available to Louisiana high school graduates who are U.S. citizens. Students must be enrolled or planning to enroll in a college, university or vocational school in Louisiana. Applicants must be full time undergraduate students and submit the Application for Federal Student Aid to be considered. Write to the above address for further information.

Louisiana Tuition Assistance Plan (TAP)
Amount: Tuition
Deadline: April 1
College Major: All Majors
Requirements: Funds are available to Louisiana residents who are U.S. citizens and are enrolled or planning to enroll in a college, university or vocational school in Louisiana. Applicants must be full time undergraduate students and demonstrate financial need. Students must fill out the Application for Federal Student Aid, to be considered. Write to the above address for further information.

Maine

Maine Education Assistance Division (Blaine House Scholars Loan)
State House Station 119
One Weston Court
Augusta, ME 04330
Amount: Up to $6000.00
Deadline: March 15
College Major: All Majors
Requirements: Loans are available to Maine residents who are high school graduates, college students or certified teachers. High school seniors must be in the top 50% of their class, a college student must be a Maine resident for at least five years and have a g.p.a. of 3.50 or higher, and a teacher must teach in a school in Maine on at least a half time basis. Write for more information.

Maine Education Assistance Division (Higher Education Interest-Free Loans)
Amount: $1500.00 per year

Deadline: March 1
College Major: All Majors
Requirements: Interest-free loans are available to Maine resident high school seniors, college students, or teachers. The loans are awarded on competitive basis with academic major and grades taken into consideration. Write for more information.

Maine Education Assistance Division (Indian Scholarships)
Amount: Varies
Deadline: Varies
College Major: All Majors
Requirements: Scholarships are open to members of the Passamaquoddy and Penobscot Tribes or Maine residents who have a parent or grandparent on the census of a North American Indian Tribe. Please write for application and more information.

Maine Education Assistance Division (Maine Student Incentive Scholarship Program)
Amount: Varies
Deadline: May 1
College Major: All Majors
Requirements: Students enrolled in New England colleges and universities that are Maine residents are eligible for these scholarships. Funds are for support of full-time undergraduate work. Write to the Finance Authority of Maine at the above address for more information.

Maine Education Assistance Division (National Science Scholars Program)
Amount: $5000.00
Deadline: October 15
College Major: Physical Science/ Computer Science/ Mathematics/ Engineering
Requirements: Scholarships are awarded to outstanding graduating high school seniors. Applicant must be a resident of Maine and have gone to school in Maine. Please write for application and more information.

Maine Education Assistance Division (Paul Douglas Teacher Scholarship Program)
Amount: $5000.00
Deadline: May 1
College Major: Education
Requirements: Scholarship is open to graduating high school seniors and undergraduate students who are planning to pursue teaching as a career. Selection is based on academic performance and merit. Recipients must fulfill teaching requirements after graduation or the awards must be repaid. Please write for application and more information.

Maine Education Assistance Division (Robert C. Byrd Honors Scholarship Program)
Amount: $1500.00
Deadline: April 15
College Major: All Majors
Requirements: Scholarships are open to graduating high school seniors in Maine. Selection is based on academic achievement and merit only. Please write for application and more information.

Maine Education Assistance Division (Student Incentive Scholarships)
Amount: $500.00 to $1000.00
Deadline: May 1
College Major: All Majors
Requirements: Scholarships are available to Maine residents who are enrolled in an accredited two or four year college, university or nursing school. Write for more information.

Maine Education Assistance Division (Tuition for Children of Firefighters and Law Enforcement Officers Killed in The Line of Duty)
Amount: Varies
Deadline: Varies
College Major: All Majors
Requirements: Scholarships are open to students attending school in the University of Maine System and Maine Maritime Academy who are children of firefighters and law enforcement officers who have been killed in the line of duty. Please write for application and more information.

Maine Education Assistance Division (Supplemental Education Loan Program)
Amount: $2000.00 to $20000.00
Deadline: Open
College Major: All Majors
Requirements: Loans are available to residents of Maine attending accredited colleges or universities. Selection is income and credit based. Please write for application and more information.

Maryland

Maryland Higher Education Commission (Child Care Provider)
16 Francis Street
Annapolis, MD 21401-1781
Amount: $500.00 to $2000.00
Deadline: June 30
College Major: Child Care
Requirements: Funds are awarded to full time and part time undergraduate students who are Maryland residents. Applicants must be enrolled in an accredited child care program at any college or university in the state. Recipients must agree to serve in the child care profession for every year the award was received. Write for more information.

Maryland Higher Education Commission (Family Practice Medical)
Amount: $7500.00
Deadline: April 15
College Major: Medicine
Requirements: Funds are awarded to full time graduate medical students who are Maryland residents. Applicants must be attending the University of Maryland at Baltimore and agree to work in family practice one year in the state for every year the award is received. Write for more information.

Maryland Higher Education Commission (General State Scholarships)
Amount: $200.00 to $2500.00
Deadline: March 1
College Major: All Majors
Requirements: Funds are awarded to full time undergraduate students who are Maryland residents. Applicants must be attending or planning to attend an accredited college or university in the state. Scholarships are renewable. Write for more information.

Maryland Higher Education Commission (Nursing Scholarship)
Amount: Up to $2400.00
Deadline: June 30
College Major: Nursing
Requirements: Funds are awarded to full time and part time nursing students who are Maryland residents. Applicants must be enrolled in an accredited nursing program at any college or university in

the state. Recipients must agree to serve in the profession for one year in the state after graduation. Write for more information.

Maryland Higher Education Commission (Part-time Grant Program)
Amount: $200.00 to $1000.00
Deadline: Varies
College Major: All Majors
Requirements: Funds are awarded to part time undergraduate students who are Maryland residents. Applicants must be enrolled in an accredited college or university in the state. Awards are renewable. Write for more information.

Maryland Higher Education Commission (Physical/Occupational Therapists & Assistance)
Amount: $2000.00
Deadline: July 1
College Major: Physical/Occupational Therapy
Requirements: Funds are awarded to full time undergraduate students who are Maryland residents. Applicants must be pursuing a career in the above areas, and be working towards certification in the state. Recipients must agree to work in the state for every year the award is received. Write for more information.

Maryland Higher Education Commission (Professional Scholarships)
Amount: $200.00 to $1000.00
Deadline: March 1
College Major: Nursing
Requirements: Funds are awarded to full time undergraduate and graduate nursing students who are Maryland residents. Applicants must be enrolled in an accredited nursing program at any college or university in the state. Awards are renewable. Write for more information.

Maryland Higher Education Commission State Scholarship Administration (Jack F. Tolbert Memorial Grant Program)
Amount: $200.00 to $1500.00
Deadline: Varies
College Major: Vocational/Technical
Requirements: Funds are available to residents of the state of Maryland who are interested in pursuing a vocational or technical career. Write to the above address for more information.

Maryland Higher Education Commission State Scholarship Administration (Edward T Conroy Memorial Scholarship Program)
Amount: Tuition
Deadline: Varies
College Major: All Majors
Requirements: Scholarships are open to the children, ages 16 to 23 , whose parents are residents of Maryland prior to entering the Armed Forces. Parents must have died or been disabled during war or MIA or POW. Applicant must be a US citizen or legal resident. Award is for undergraduate or graduate study in the US. Scholarships are renewable for eight years. Write for information.

Maryland Higher Education Commission State Scholarship Administration (House of Delegate Scholarships)
Amount: Varies
Deadline: Varies
College Major: All Majors

Requirements: Funds are available to students who live in a district where a member of the House of Delegates resides. Applicants must be US citizens or legal residents and plan to pursue an undergraduate or graduate degree in any accredited institution nationwide. Write for more information.

Maryland Higher Education Commission State Scholarship Administration (Senatorial Scholarship Program)
Amount: $400.00 to $2000.00
Deadline: March 1
College Major: All Majors
Requirements: Funds are available to students pursuing an undergraduate or graduate degree in any accredited institution nationwide. Applicants must be residents of Maryland. Students who are hearing-impaired are encouraged to apply. Contact the address above for more information.

Maryland Higher Education Commission State Scholarship Admin (Children of Deceased Firemen/Police/Natl Guard/Correctional Officer)
Amount: $700.00 to $1000.00
Deadline: March 2
College Major: All Majors
Requirements: Students whose parent(s) were correctional officers, firemen, members of the national guard, policemen, or rescue squad members who were killed while serving in the state of Maryland, are eligible to receive these funds. Applicants must be 16-23 years old and enrolled in an accredited college or university in the state, and pursuing an undergraduate or graduate degree. Write for more information.

Maryland Higher Education Commission State Scholarship Administration (Paul Douglas Teacher Scholarship)
Amount: Up to $5000.00
Deadline: March 31
College Major: Education
Requirements: US citizens or legal residents who are also Maryland residents and rank in the top tenth of their high school class or the top tenth on GED scores are eligible for these funds. Recipients must agree to teach in a public or private nonprofit school or program for two years for every year of financial assistance. The awards are renewable. Write for more information.

Maryland Higher Education Commission State Scholarship Administration (Teacher Education Distinguished Scholar Award)
Amount: $3000.00
Deadline: None
College Major: Education
Requirements: There are approximately 30 merit based scholarships available to Distinguished Scholar recipients attending a Maryland school with a teacher education program. Recipients can renew the funds annually as long as they maintain a 3.0 g.p.a. and agree to teach one year in a Maryland public school for each year of financial help. Write for more information.

Maryland Higher Education Commission State Scholarship Administration (Sharon Christa McAuliffe Memorial Teacher Education Award)
Amount: Varies
Deadline: December 31
College Major: Education
Requirements: Funds are available to college students planning to enroll in a teacher certification program to become a teacher in a designated area where there is a shortage. Awards are also granted to already certified teachers who are planning to teach in an area of critical shortage. Applicant must have

a g.p.a. of 3.0 or higher and be enrolled in an accredited college or university in Maryland. Write to the above address for more information.

Maryland Higher Education Commission State Scholarships Administration (Distinguished Scholar Award)
Amount: $3000.00
Deadline: March 2
College Major: All Majors
Requirements: Scholarships are available to high school graduates who are residents of Maryland. Applicants must be Achievement or National Merit Finalists and plan to pursue an undergraduate degree at an accredited institution in Maryland. Write for more information.

Massachusetts

Massachusetts American Student Assistance (Christa McAuliffe Teacher Incentive Grant)
330 Stuart Street
Boston, MA 02116
Amount: Varies
Deadline: None
College Major: Education
Requirements: Scholarships are available to Massachusetts resident undergraduate college students who are Massachusetts institution. Write for more information.

Massachusetts American Student Assistance (Family Education Loan)
Amount: Tuition
Deadline: None
College Major: All Majors
Requirements: Loans are available to Massachusetts resident college students. Write for more information and application details.

Massachusetts American Student Assistance (Gilbert Matching Scholarship)
Amount: Varies
Deadline: None
College Major: All Majors
Requirements: Scholarships are available to Massachusetts resident full time college students who are attending a Massachusetts independent college or university. Write for more information.

Massachusetts American Student Assistance (Graduate Grant)
Amount: Varies
Deadline: None
College Major: All Majors
Requirements: Scholarships are available to Massachusetts resident graduate students who are full time students in a Massachusetts institution. Write for more information.

Massachusetts American Student Assistance (Help Loans)
Amount: $2500.00 undergraduate; $5000.00 graduates
Deadline: None
College Major: All Majors
Requirements: US citizens who are permanent residents of Massachusetts are eligible to apply. Applicants must be enrolled and in good standing or accepted at least half time at an approved institution. Applicants must qualify for eligibility under ASA criteria. Approximately 125000 loans are awarded per year.

Massachusetts American Student Assistance (Part Time Student Grant)
Amount: Varies
Deadline: None
College Major: All Majors
Requirements: Grants are available to Massachusetts residents who are part time college students at a Massachusetts institution of higher learning. Write for more information.

Massachusetts American Student Assistance (Paul Douglas Teacher Scholarship)
Amount: Up to $5000.00
Deadline: None
College Major: Education
Requirements: Scholarships are available to Massachusetts resident college students who are pursuing the above major. Write for more information.

Massachusetts American Student Assistance (Public Service Scholarship)
Amount: $750.00
Deadline: None
College Major: All Majors
Requirements: Scholarships are available to Massachusetts residents who are children of deceased fire or police officers or veterans. Write for more information.

Massachusetts American Student Assistance (State General Scholarship)
Amount: $200.00 to $3800.00
Deadline: January 1 to May 1
College Major: All Majors
Requirements: Scholarships are available to Massachusetts resident full time college students. Applicants can only qualify if they are enrolled in a college or university in Connecticut, Maine, Maryland, New Hampshire, Pennsylvania, Rhode Island or Washington, D.C. Write for more information.

Massachusetts American Student Assistance (Tuition Wavier)
Amount: Tuition
Deadline: None
College Major: All Majors
Requirements: Scholarships are available to Massachusetts residents who are attending a Massachusetts public school. Write for more information.

Michigan
Michigan Department of Education (Michigan Competitive Scholarships)
Student Financial Assistance Services
P.O. Box 30008
Lansing, MI 48909
Amount: $1200.00
Deadline: February 15 (high school) March 15 (college)
College Major: All Majors
Requirements: US citizens and residents of Michigan for at least one year who are full time undergraduates at a Michigan collegiate institution are eligible for these renewable scholarships. Students must submit ACT scores and prove financial need. Write for more information.

Michigan Department of Education (Michigan Tuition Grants)
Amount: $1900.00
Deadline: September 1
College Major: All Majors

Requirements: Grants for Michigan residents who are full time students at independent non-profit Michigan institutions and show financial need. For more information contact the above address.

Minnesota

Minnesota Higher Education Coordinating Board (Academic Excellence Scholarship)
400 Capitol Square Building
550 Cedar Street
St. Paul, MN 55101
Amount: State Tuition and Fees
Deadline: None
College Major: English/Creative Writing/Fine Arts/Foreign Language/Math/Science/Social Science
Requirements: Scholarships are available to Minnesota resident high school graduates who are studying one of the above fields of study. Applicants must be enrolled in a Minnesota public or private college or university. Write for more information.

Minnesota Higher Education Coordinating Board (Dislocated Rural Workers Grant)
Amount: Varies
Deadline: None
College Major: Agriculture/Farm Management
Requirements: Grants are available to Minnesota residents registered in a farm management school who are unemployed or will soon be unemployed or are farmers who need financial assistance. Write for more information.

Minnesota Higher Education Coordinating Board (Farm Families/University of Minnesota Department of Agriculture Scholarships)
Amount: Partial Tuition Waivers
Deadline: February 1
College Major: Agriculture
Requirements: Scholarships are available to Minnesota resident farmers who are in danger of foreclosure of their family farm. Applicants must be high school graduates, have a minimum g.p.a. of 3.5, be in the top 10% of their high school class, and attend a Minnesota State college or University. Write for more information.

Minnesota Higher Education Coordinating Board (Minnesota Child Care Grant)
Amount: Varies
Deadline: None
College Major: All Majors
Requirements: Grants are available to Minnesota resident undergraduate college students who have a child that is no older than 12 or a handicapped child that is no older than 14. Write for more information.

Minnesota Higher Education Coordinating Board (Minnesota State Grant Program)
Amount: Up to $5889.00
Deadline: May 2
College Major: All Majors
Requirements: Scholarships are available to Minnesota resident undergraduate college students attending school full- or part-time. Write for more information.

Minnesota Higher Education Coordinating Board (National Science Scholars Program)
Amount: $5000.00
Deadline: None
College Major: Physical Life/Computer Sciences/Mathematics/ Engineering
Requirements: Scholarships are available to Minnesota resident undergraduates or high school seniors who are skilled in one of the above fields of study. Write for more information.

Minnesota Higher Education Coordinating Board (Native American Scholarship)
Amount: $1450.00
Deadline: None
College Major: All Majors
Requirements: Scholarships are available to Minnesota residents who are members of an Indian tribe that is recognized by the Minnesota government. Applicants must be high school graduates who plan to attend a Minnesota college or university. Write for more information.

Minnesota Higher Education Coordinating Board (Nursing Grants)
Amount: $500.00 to $2500.00
Deadline: August 1
College Major: Nursing
Requirements: Grants are available to Minnesota resident nursing students. Recipient must agree to serve at least three years following licensure in a designated rural area. Write for more information.

Minnesota Higher Education Coordinating Board (Paul Douglas Teacher Scholarship)
Amount: Up to $5000.00
Deadline: None
College Major: Education
Requirements: Scholarships are available to Minnesota resident high school graduates who plan to pursue a career in teaching. Applicants must be US citizens and full time students who graduated in the upper 10% of their class. Write for additional information.

Minnesota Higher Education Coordinating Board (Robert C. Byrd Honors Scholarship)
Amount: $1500.00
Deadline: March 1
College Major: All Majors
Requirements: Scholarships are available to Minnesota high school students. Write for more information.

Minnesota Higher Education Coordinating Board (Safety Officers' Survivor Program)
Amount: Tuition and Fees
Deadline: None
College Major: All Majors
Requirements: Scholarships are available to children and spouses of deceased Minnesota safety officers who were killed while in service after January 1, 1973. Applicants must plan to attend a Minnesota college or university. Please write for more information.

Minnesota Higher Education Coordinating Board (Scholarships and Grants)
Amount: $100.00 to $5889.00
Deadline: May 31
College Major: All Majors
Requirements: There are unlimited scholarships and grants awarded yearly to Minnesota residents (who are also U.S. citizens) attending state colleges or universities. Please write for complete information.

Minnesota Higher Education Coordinating Board (Student Educational Loans)
Amount: $1000.00 to $25000.00
Deadline: None
College Major: All Majors
Requirements: Loans are available to Minnesota resident college students. Write for more application details.

Minnesota Higher Education Coordinating Board (Student Loan Program)
Amount: $2625.00 to $4000.00 per year (undergraduate); $7500.00 per year (graduate)

Deadline: Five weeks before enrollment period
College Major: All Majors
Requirements: Residents of Minnesota or non-residents attending an eligible Minnesota school may apply as long as they can show financial need and prove U.S. citizenship. Approximately 10,000 loans are awarded each year. Please write for more information.

Minnesota Higher Education Coordinating Board (Summer Scholarships for Academic Enrichment)
Amount: Up to $1000.00
Deadline: None
College Major: All Majors
Requirements: Scholarships are available to Minnesota resident students who have not graduated from high school yet. Must have above average grades and financial need. Write for more information.

Minnesota Higher Education Coordinating Board (Supplemental Educational Opportunity Grant Program)
Amount: $4000.00
Deadline: Varies
College Major: All Majors
Requirements: This grant adds money to a financial aid package that has been already received by a student. Demonstrated financial need is necessary. Write to the above address for more information.

Minnesota Higher Education Coordinating Board (Veterans' Dependents Assistance)
Amount: Tuition
Deadline: None
College Major: All Majors
Requirements: Scholarships are available to children of individuals declared to be prisoners of war or missing in action prior to August 1, 1958. Write for information.

Minnesota Higher Education Coordinating Board (Veterans Education Assistance Program)
Amount: Up to $2700.00
Deadline: None
College Major: All Majors
Requirements: Funds are available to Minnesota state resident veterans who entered the Armed Forces from January 1, 1977 to June 30, 1985. Write for more information.

Mississippi
Mississippi Board of Trustees of State Institutions of Higher Learning (State Student Incentive Grant)
3825 Ridgewood Road
Jackson, MS 39211-6463
Amount: $200.00 to $1500.00
Deadline: None
College Major: All Majors
Requirements: Grants are available to full time undergraduate students who are Mississippi residents. Applicants must demonstrate financial need. Applications must be filed at the student's school. Write for more information.

Mississippi Board of Trustees of State Institution of Higher Learning (Nursing Education Scholarship Grants)
Amount: $1500.00 to $10000.00
Deadline: March 31 & July 7

College Major: Nursing
Requirements: Scholarships are open to Mississippi residents (at least one year). Applicants can be currently licensed as a registered nurse in Mississippi or admitted to an accredited Bachelor of Science Degree Nursing program or a graduate degree program. Scholarships are renewable. Write for complete details.

Mississippi Board of Trustees of State Institution of Higher Learning (Graduate & Professional Program)
Amount: $5000.00
Deadline: June 30
College Major: Health Related/Podiatric Medicine
Requirements: Scholarships are available to Mississippi residents that wish to receive a professional degree not available at Mississippi institutions. Renewable for up to three years. Student must give service in the field in Mississippi for one year for every one year's award. If the service is not carried out the scholarships become loans. Write for more information.

Mississippi Board of Trustees of State Institution of Higher Learning (Academic Common Market Program)
Amount: Varies
Deadline: Open
College Major: All Majors
Requirements: This program offers in-state tuition to out-of-state residents pursuing degrees not offered in their home state. Many southern states participate. Awards are not repaid. Write for more information.

Mississippi Board of Trustees of State Institution of Higher Learning (SREB Loan/Scholarship Program)
Amount: Varies
Deadline: June 30
College Major: Optometry/Osteopathic Medicine
Requirements: Scholarships are available to Mississippi residents pursuing one of the two degrees listed above. Awards are available for up to four years. Student must give one year's service in Mississippi for every year of award. Write to the above address for more information.

Mississippi Board of Trustees of State Institutions of Higher Learning (Math-Science Teacher Education Scholarship Program)
Amount: Up to $3000.00 per year
Deadline: Varies
College Major: Math/Science Education
Requirements: Scholarships are available to full time students who are enrolled at the junior or senior level in a state college or university in a teacher education program striving for a Class A certification in math and or science. Recipients are obligated to teach in a critical teacher shortage area in Mississippi after graduation. Please write for application and more information.

Mississippi Board of Trustees of State Institutions of Higher Learning (Law Enforcement Officers and Firemen Scholarships)
Amount: Tuition
Deadline: Varies
College Major: All Majors
Requirements: Scholarships are offered to the children of law enforcement officers and full time firemen who were killed or disabled on duty. Applicants must be under 23 years of age. Awards cover tuition for eight semesters at all state supported Mississippi schools. Write for more information.

Mississippi Board of Trustees of State Institutions of Higher Learning (Southeast Asia POW/MIA Scholarship Program)
Amount: Tuition
Deadline: Varies
College Major: All Majors
Requirements: Children of Southeast Asia veterans who were officially reported as a POW or MIA. Awards are for eight semesters of tuition at all Mississippi state supported schools. Write for more information.

Mississippi Office of State Student Financial Aid (African-American Doctoral Teacher Scholarship Program)
Amount: $10000.00
Deadline: June 30
College Major: Education
Requirements: Scholarships are open to African-American students who are Mississippi residents who are enrolled in a doctoral program at a recognized institution in Mississippi. Applicant must be planning to teach in a college or university in Mississippi. Please write for application and more information.

Mississippi Office of State Student Financial Aid (Graduate & Professional Degree Scholarship Program)
Amount: $5000.00
Deadline: June 30
College Major: Health Related Fields
Requirements: Scholarships are open to residents of Mississippi who are pursuing a degree not available at a Mississippi university. Applicant must be enrolled in a recognized out of state college or university. Please write for application and more information.

Mississippi Office of State Student Financial Aid (Nursing Education Scholarship Program)
Amount: Varies
Deadline: Varies
College Major: Nursing
Requirements: Scholarships are open to Mississippi residents who are pursuing a career in nursing. Applicant must have at least a 2.5 g.p.a.. Please write for application and more information.

Mississippi Office of State Student Financial Aid (Paul Douglas Teacher Scholarship Program)
Amount: $5000.00
Deadline: March 31
College Major: Education
Requirements: Scholarships are open to Mississippi residents who are enrolled in a program leading to a teaching certificate. Applicant must have graduated in the top 10% of his or her class. Selection is based on academic performance and commitment to the teaching profession. Please write for application and more information.

Mississippi Office of State Student Financial Aid (Special Medical Education Scholarship Program)
Amount: $24000.00
Deadline: June 30
College Major: Medicine
Requirements: Scholarships are open to students enrolled at the University of Mississippi School of Medicine. Selection is based on academic performance and financial need. Please write for application and more information.

Mississippi Office of State Student Financial Aid (State Dental Education Scholarship Program)
Amount: $4000.00
Deadline: June 30
College Major: Dentistry
Requirements: Scholarships are open to Mississippi residents who have been accepted to the University of Mississippi School of Dentistry. Please write for application and more information.

Mississippi Office of State Student Financial Aid (William Winter Teacher Scholar Program)
Amount: $1000.00 to $3000.00
Deadline: March 31
College Major: Education
Requirements: Scholarships are open to Mississippi residents who are enrolled full time in a teaching certification program. Applicant must have at least a 2.5 g.p.a.. Recipients are obligated to teach in a critical shortage area for the number of years aid was received. Please write for application and more information.

Mississippi Office of State Students Financial Aid (Southern Regional Education Board Scholarship Program)
Amount: Varies
Deadline: June 30
College Major: Optometry/ Osteopathic Medicine
Requirements: Scholarships are open to residents of Mississippi enrolled in accredited programs in the above areas. Please write for application and more information.

Missouri
Missouri Coordinating Board for Higher Education (Higher Education Academic Scholarship Program)
P.O. Box 1438
Jefferson City, MO 65102
Amount: $2000.00
Deadline: June 1
College Major: All Majors
Requirements: Missouri and US residents who are accepted for full time undergraduate study are eligible to apply. Applicants must have a composite ACT or SAT score in the top 3% for Missouri schools. Undergraduate scholarships are renewable each year that a recipient is an undergraduate. Please write at the above address for complete information.

Missouri Coordinating Board for Higher Education (Missouri Prospective Teacher Scholarship Program)
Amount: $500.00 to $1000.00
Deadline: June 1
College Major: Education
Requirements: This program is open to Missouri residents only. Applicant must be an undergraduate upperclassman, a US citizen and is need of financial aid. Loans need not be repaid if recipient teaches in areas of critical need in Missouri after graduation. Please write for application and more information.

Missouri Coordinating Board for Higher Education (Missouri Public Service Officer or Employee's Child Survivor Grant)
Amount: Varies
Deadline: None
College Major: All Majors

Requirements: Grants are available for the dependents of public safety officers or employees of the Department of Highways and Transportation who died in the line of duty. Applicant must be accepted or enrolled as a full time undergraduate student at an institution in Missouri and be under the age of 24 years. Please write for application and more information.

Missouri Coordinating Board for Higher Education (Missouri Student Grant Program)
Amount: $100.00 to $1500.00
Deadline: January 1 to April 30
College Major: All Majors
Requirements: 8300 grants are available to undergraduates who are residents of Missouri and the US. Applicants must submit a state FAF or FFS form. Write for more information.

Missouri Coordinating Board for Higher Education (Paul Douglas Teacher Scholarship)
Amount: Up to $5000.00
Deadline: None
College Major: Education
Requirements: Scholarships are available to Missouri state residents who are pursuing an education in teaching. Applicants must be high school students who are graduating in the top 10% of their class. US citizens only please. Write for more information.

Montana

Montana Guaranteed Student Loan Program (Bureau of Indian Affairs Loans and Tribal Loans)
2500 Broadway
Helena, MT 59620-3104
Amount: Varies
Deadline: Varies
College Major: All Majors
Requirements: Loans are available to Native American students. Applicant must demonstrate financial need. Please write for application and more information.

Montana Guaranteed Student Loan Program (Health Education Assistance Loan)
Amount: Varies
Deadline: Varies
College Major: Dentistry/ Medicine/ Optometry/ Veterinary Medicine/ Pharmacy/ Psychology/ Health Administration
Requirements: Loans are available to students enrolled in programs in the above areas. Please write for application and more information.

Montana Guaranteed Student Loan Program (Nursing Student Loan Program)
Amount: $10000.00
Deadline: Varies
College Major: Nursing
Requirements: Loans are available to part time and full time nursing students attending accredited schools in the US. Please write for application and more information.

Nebraska

Nebraska Coordinating Commission for Post-secondary Education (Post-secondary Education Award Program-PEAP)
P.O. Box 95005
Lincoln, NE 68509-5005
Amount: Varies

Deadline: None
College Major: All Majors
Requirements: Scholarships are available to Nebraska resident college students who are enrolled in a Nebraska Post-secondary institution. Write for more information.

Nebraska Coordinating Commission for Post-secondary Education (Health Professions Student Loans for Medicine, Dentistry, and Pharmacy)
Amount: Up to $2500.00 + Tuition and Fees
Deadline: None
College Major: Medicine/Dentistry/Pharmacy
Requirements: Loans are available to students who are studying in one of the above fields of study. Must be a US citizen and exhibit financial aid. Write for more information.

Nebraska Coordinating Commission for Post-secondary Education (Veterans' Benefits)
Amount: Tuition
Deadline: None
College Major: All Majors
Requirements: Scholarships are available to Nebraska state residents who are children or spouses of deceased or permanently and totally disabled veterans. Must exhibit financial need. Write for more information.

Nebraska Coordination Commission for Post-secondary Education (Nursing Student Loan Program-NSL)
Amount: $2500.00
Deadline: None
College Major: Nursing
Requirements: Loans are available to college students who are studying the above field of study and is a US citizen, enrolled in an accredited nursing program, and is financially needy. Write for more information.

Nebraska Coordination Commission for Post-secondary Education (Medical Student Loan Program)
Amount: Up to $5000.00
Deadline: None
College Major: Medicine
Requirements: Loans are available to Nebraska resident medical students who are enrolled in a medical program at either Creighton University or the University of Nebraska. Write for more information.

Nevada

Nevada Student Aid Services (Nevada Resident Grant-in-Aid)
The Scholarship Office-(706)
University of Nevada-Reno
Reno, NV 89557
Amount: $500.00
Deadline: June 1
College Major: All Majors
Requirements: Grants are available to Nevada state residents who are seeking financial aid. Awards are based on financial aid, a minimum g.p.a. of 2.0, and class standing. Must be a full time student. Write for more information.

Nevada Student Aid Services (Out of State Grant in Aid)
Amount: $416.25

Deadline: June 1
College Major: All Majors
Requirements: Grants are available to residents of particular California counties bordering Nevada. Awards are based on financial aid, class standing, and a minimum g.p.a. of 3.0. Write for more information.

New Hampshire

New Hampshire Post-Secondary Education Commission (Federal Family Education Loan Program Parent and Auxiliary Loans)
P.O. Box 877
Concord, NH 03302
Amount: Varies
Deadline: None
College Major: All Majors
Requirements: Applicants must be US citizens and residents of New Hampshire to be eligible for assistance. Applicants must also be enrolled or be planning to enroll in an accredited post-secondary school, in good academic standing and in need of financial assistance. Please write for complete information.

New Hampshire Post-Secondary Education Commission (Nursing Education Assistance Grants)
Two Industrial Park Drive
Concord, NH 03301-8512
Amount: $150.00 to $2000.00
Deadline: June 1& January 1 & May 1
College Major: Nursing
Requirements: New Hampshire residents admitted to or registered in a recognized nursing program in the state of New Hampshire are eligible for these grants. Applicants must be US citizens or legal residents. There are 110 grants awarded per year. Recipients must practice nursing in New Hampshire one year for every year they receive the awards. Write for more information.

New Hampshire Post-secondary Education Commission (Incentive Grants)
Amount: $100.00 to $2000.00
Deadline: May 1
College Major: All Majors
Requirements: Grants are awarded to New Hampshire residents who are enrolled or planning to enroll in a college or university in New Hampshire. Applicants must demonstrate financial need. Write to the above address for more information.

New Hampshire Post-secondary Education Commission (Paul Douglas Teacher Scholarship)
Amount: $5000.00 per year
Deadline: May 1
College Major: Education
Requirements: Scholarships are awarded to high school graduates in the top 10% of their class who are New Hampshire residents. Applicants must be enrolled at an accredited college or university and planning to pursue a career in education. Write to the above address for more information.

New Hampshire Post-secondary Education Commission (Robert C. Byrd Honors Scholarships)
Amount: $1500.00
Deadline: Varies
College Major: All Majors

Requirements: Funds are available to New Hampshire residents who have graduated from a high school in the state and are enrolled or will be enrolling in an accredited college or university. The grant is not renewable. Write to the above address for more information.

New Hampshire Post-secondary Education Commission (Scholarships for Orphans of Veterans)
Amount: $1000.00
Deadline: None
College Major: All Majors
Requirements: Scholarships are available to the children whose parents died as a result of service in World War I and II, Korea, and Southeast Asia. Applicants must be New Hampshire residents and their parents must have been residents at the time of death. Tuition and fees are paid at any institution of higher education in the state. Write to the above address for more information.

New Jersey
New Jersey Department of Higher Education (Distinguished Scholars Program)
Office of Student Assistance
CN 540
Trenton, NJ 08625
Amount: $1000.00
Deadline: Fall
College Major: All Majors
Requirements: Applicants must be U.S. citizens or legal residents and residents of New Jersey. The program is open to high school students with academic excellence who plan to attend a New Jersey school. Do not apply directly to the program. Applications must be acquired through your high school. Please contact high school guidance counselor or the given address for complete information.

New Jersey Department of Higher Education (Garden State Scholarships)
Amount: $500.00
Deadline: March 1
College Major: All Majors
Requirements: Residents of New Jersey who demonstrate financial need and scholastic achievement and are US citizens or legal residents are eligible to apply for this award. The undergraduate awards are renewable. Please write for more complete information.

New Jersey Department of Higher Education (Higher Education Loan Program) NJHEA
Amount: Partial or full tuition
Deadline: October 1; March 1
College Major: All Majors
Requirements: New Jersey residents who are dependents of emergency service personnel or law officers killed in the line of duty in New Jersey are eligible to apply. Applicants must be U.S. citizens or legal residents. The grant awards are renewable. Please write for complete information.

New Jersey Department of Higher Education (POW/MIA Dependent's Grant)
Amount: Tuition
Deadline: October 1; March 1
College Major: All Majors
Requirements: Grants offered to New Jersey residents who are the children of U.S. Military personnel who were declared POWs or MIAs after January 1, 1960. Awards for undergraduate study only. Write for more information.

New Jersey Department of Higher Education (Public Tuition Benefit Program)
Amount: Tuition
Deadline: October 1 & March 1

College Major: All Majors
Requirements: The children of emergency service personnel or law officers killed in the line of duty in New Jersey are eligible to apply. Applicants must be New Jersey and U.S. citizens (or legal residents). Awards for undergraduate study only. Grants are renewable. Write for more information.

New Jersey Department of Higher Education (Supplemental Educational Opportunity Grants)
Amount: Varies
Deadline: October 1; March 1
College Major: All Majors
Requirements: New Jersey residents are eligible to apply for grants designed for economically and educationally disadvantaged students. Grants are for undergraduate or graduate study in New Jersey and they are renewable. Applicants must be U.S. citizens or legal residents and demonstrate financial need. Please write for complete information.

New Jersey Department of Higher Education (Tuition Aid Grants)
Amount: $200.00 to $3000.00
Deadline: October 1; March 1
College Major: All Majors
Requirements: New Jersey residents who plan to enroll full time in undergraduate study at any college or university in New Jersey are eligible to apply. Applicants must be U.S. citizens or legal residents. Grants are renewable. Write for more information.

New Jersey Department of Higher Education (Veterans Tuition Credit Program)
Amount: $400.00
Deadline: October 1; March 1
College Major: All Majors
Requirements: This program helps Veterans who served between December 31, 1960 and August 1, 1974 to finance tuition. Qualifying veterans must have been residents of New Jersey at the time of induction or discharge. Contact the above address for more information.

New Jersey Department of Higher Education (Vietnam Veterans Tuition Aid Program)
Amount: Tuition
Deadline: October 1; March 1
College Major: All Majors
Requirements: Scholarships are open to New Jersey residents who are Vietnam Veterans living in New Jersey since April 9, 1983. Awards are for undergraduate study only. Write for more information.

New Mexico
New Mexico Educational Assistance Foundation (Athlete Scholarship Program)
3900 Osuna NE
P.O. Box 27020
Albuquerque, NM 87125-7020
Amount: Varies
Deadline: Varies
College Major: All Majors
Requirements: Scholarships are open to athletes attending one of the following school in New Mexico: University of New Mexico, New Mexico State University, Eastern New Mexico University, New Mexico Highlands University, Western New Mexico University and New Mexico Junior College. Please write for application and more information.

New Mexico Educational Assistance Foundation (Graduate Scholarships)
Amount: $7200.00 per year
Deadline: Varies

College Major: Business/Engineering/Computer Science/ Mathematics/Agriculture
Requirements: Applicants must be graduate students in the state of New Mexico, U.S. citizens, and residents of New Mexico state. Recipients will serve an unpaid, ten-hour per week internship or assistantship. These fellowships are awarded on a yearly basis, and may be renewed.

New Mexico Educational Assistance Foundation (Minority Doctoral Assistance)
Amount: Varies
Deadline:
College Major: All Majors
Requirements: Qualified applicants must be US citizens and residents of New Mexico state. Applicants must have completed the requirements for a baccalaureate or master's degree at a four-year public institution in New Mexico, and have gained acceptance as a full-time doctorate student in an out-of-state institution. Please write for additional information.

New Mexico Educational Assistance Foundation (New Mexico Scholars Program)
Amount: Tuition and Fees
Deadline: None
College Major: All Majors
Requirements: Scholarships are available to New Mexico resident high school graduates who plan to enroll as full time students in a New Mexico college or university. Applicants must be U.S. citizens and score a 1020 on the SAT or a 25 on the ACT. Write for more information.

New Mexico Educational Assistance Foundation (Nursing Student Loan)
Amount: Up to $10000.00
Deadline: None
College Major: Nursing
Requirements: Loans are available to New Mexico resident nursing students. Applicants must be US citizens. Write for more information.

New Mexico Educational Assistance Foundation (Osteopathic Medical Student Loan)
Amount: Varies
Deadline:
College Major: Osteopathic Medicine
Requirements: Qualified applicants must be US citizens and residents of New Mexico state. Recipients of loan must be accepted into an accredited Osteopathic doctorate program, and declare their intention to establish a full-time practice in New Mexico. Loans are based on financial need and may be repaid through services rendered. Please write for additional information.

New Mexico Educational Assistance Foundation (Physician Student Loan)
Amount: Varies
Deadline: Varies
College Major: Medicine
Requirements: Qualified applicants must be U.S. citizens and residents of New Mexico state. Recipients must be enrolled in an accredited doctoral medical program in the United States, and must declare their intention to establish a full-time practice New Mexico. Loans are awarded based on the Need Analysis Form, and may be repaid through service. Please write for additional information.

New Mexico Educational Assistance Foundation (Student Choice Grants)
Amount: Varies
Deadline: None
College Major: All Majors

Requirements: Grants are available to New Mexico college students attending the College of Santa Fe, St. John's College in Santa Fe, or the College of the Southwest in Hobbs. Applicants must be U.S. citizens. Write for more information.

New Mexico Educational Assistance Foundation (Student Incentive Grant)
Amount: $2000.00
Deadline: None
College Major: All Majors
Requirements: Grants are available to New Mexico residents who are enrolled at least half time in an undergraduate institution in New Mexico. Applicants must be US citizens or legal residents. There are 2700 grants available per year. Write for more information.

New Mexico Educational Assistance Foundation (Three Percent Scholars Program)
Amount: Varies
Deadline: Varies
College Major: All Majors
Requirements: Scholarships are open to New Mexico residents who are graduates from New Mexico high schools enrolled as a full time undergraduate student at an institution in New Mexico. Applicant must have graduated in the upper 5% of their class. Please write for application and more information.

New Mexico Educational Assistance Foundation (Vietnam Veteran's Scholarship)
Amount: Varies
Deadline: None specified
College Major: All Majors
Requirements: Qualified applicants must be certified by the New Mexico Veteran's Service as being eligible for this scholarship. Scholarships are awarded on a "first come, first served" basis. Please write for additional information.

New York
New York State Higher Education Services Corporation (Aid for Part-Time Study)
99 Washington Avenue
Albany, NY 12255
Amount: Up to $2000.00
Deadline: None specified
College Major: All Majors
Requirements: Qualified applicants must be enrolled part time in an approved undergraduate degree program in New York state, and must be a U.S. citizen or permanent resident, alien, or refugee. Applicants must meet income limits and must not have exhausted their Tuition Assistance Program eligibility. Applicants default on previous loans may not be eligible. Please write for additional information.

New York State Higher Education Services Corporation (Child of Deceased Police Officer-Firefighter-Corrections Officer Awards)
Amount: $450.00
Deadline: None specified
College Major: All Majors
Requirements: Qualified applicants must be the children of a deceased police officer, firefighter, or corrections officer. Applicants must be residents of New York state and enrolled in an approved undergraduate program at a college or university in New York state. Please write for additional information.

New York State Higher Education Services Corporation (Empire State Challenger Scholarships for Teachers—Undergraduate)
Amount: Up to $3000.00
Deadline: None
College Major: Education
Requirements: Scholarships are available to New York resident college students who are pursuing a major in teachers' education. Applicants must be U.S. citizens and attend a New York college or university. Write for more information.

New York State Higher Education Services Corporation (Empire State Challenger Fellowships for Teachers-Graduate)
Amount: $5000.00 per Year
Deadline: None specified
College Major: Education
Requirements: Qualified applicants must be either U.S. citizens or hold a permanent immigration visa or a refugee visa, and must be a New York State resident. Applicants must be enrolled in a graduate program pursuing a teaching certificate. Please write for additional information.

New York State Higher Education Services Corporation (Guaranteed Student Loan Program)
Amount: Varies
Deadline: None specified
College Major: All Majors
Requirements: Loans are available to New York residents who are enrolled at least half time at a recognized college or university in the U.S. Applicants must be U.S. citizens or legal residents. These loans are renewable. Write for more information.

New York State Higher Education Services Corporation (Memorial Scholarships for Children of Deceased Police Officers and Firefighters)
Amount: Tuition
Deadline: None
College Major: All Majors
Requirements: Scholarships are available to full time college students who are the children of deceased police officers and firefighters. Applicants must be New York residents and U.S. citizens. Write for more information.

New York State Higher Education Services Corporation (New York State Higher Education Opportunity Program)
Amount: Varies
Deadline: None
College Major: All Majors
Requirements: Scholarships are available to students who are economically and/or academically disadvantaged. Write for more information.

New York State Higher Education Services Corporation (New York State Professional Opportunity Scholarships)
Amount: $1000.00 to $5000.00
Deadline: January 15
College Major: All Majors
Requirements: Scholarships are available to New York resident college students study for an undergraduate degree. Applicants must be U.S. citizens. Write for more information.

New York State Higher Education Services Corporation (Paul Douglas Teacher Scholarship)
Amount: Up to $5000.00

Deadline: February 1
College Major: Education
Requirements: Undergraduate students are eligible for these scholarships if they are New York residents, rank in the top tenth of their class and agree to pursue a teaching certificate in a field having a shortage of teachers. Recipients may reapply for renewal and must agree to teach a specified amount of time after their schooling. Write for more information.

New York State Higher Education Services Corporation (Physician Loan Forgiveness)
Amount: Up to $40,000
Deadline: April 1
College Major: Medicine
Requirements: Qualified applicants must be U.S. citizens and a resident of New York state. Applicant must have completed residency and have graduated from a medical program in the United States or Canada registered by the State Education Department or accredited by the Liaison Committee on Medical Education or the American Osteopathic Association. Please write for additional information.

New York State Higher Education Services Corporation (Progressional Education Nursing)
Amount: $250.00 per Year
Deadline: November 5
College Major: Nursing
Requirements: Qualified applicants must be U.S. citizens, permanent residents or refugees, and New York state residents planning to become a registered professional nurse. Applicants must be a high school graduate or accepted and enrolled as a full-time student at an approved college or equivalent program. Those who were considered for a Regent's scholarship in the previous year are ineligible. Please write for additional information.

New York State Higher Education Services Corporation (Regents Grants for Children of Deceased Police Officers and Firefighters)
Amount: $450.00
Deadline: None
College Major: All Majors
Requirements: Scholarships are open to New York residents who are children of New York police officers, correction officers, firefighters or volunteer firefighters who have died on duty. Awards are given for vocational and technical training in the state of New York. Write for more information.

New York State Higher Education Services Corporation (Regents Grants for Children of Deceased or Disabled Veterans)
Amount: $450.00
Deadline: None
College Major: All Majors
Requirements: Grants are available for the children of deceased or disabled Veterans who are residents of New York. Awards are for undergraduate or vocational and technical training. Write for more information.

New York State Higher Education Services Corporation (Regents College Scholarship)
Amount: $1000.00
Deadline: November 5
College Major: All Majors
Requirements: Scholarships are available to high school graduates and New York residents who are enrolled (or plan to enroll) as full time students in a New York two or four year school program. Must be a US Citizen. Write for more information.

New York State Higher Education Services Corporation (Regents Professional Education Nursing Scholarship)
Amount: $250.00
Deadline: November 5
College Major: Nursing
Requirements: Scholarships are available to New York resident nursing students. Applicants must be US citizens. Write for more information.

New York State Higher Education Services Corporation (Robert C. Byrd Honors Scholarship)
Amount: $1500.00
Deadline: November 5
College Major: All Majors
Requirements: Scholarships are available to New York state residents who are high school graduates and plan to pursue a college degree. Applicants must be U.S. citizens. Write for more information.

New York State Higher Education Services Corporation (Scholarship at Cornell University)
Amount: $100.00 to $1000.00 per Year
Deadline: November 5
College Major: All Majors
Requirements: Qualified applicants must be U.S. citizens or permanent residents or refugees of the United States, and must meet admission requirements at Cornell University. Those considered for Regents' scholarships in the previous year are ineligible. Awards are valid for four to five years. Must have satisfactory SAT/ACT scores to apply. Please write for additional information.

New York State Higher Education Services Corporation (Tuition Assistance Program-Tap Grants)
Amount: Up to $4125.00
Deadline: May 1
College Major: All Majors
Requirements: Grants are available to New York and U.S. residents who attend either graduate or undergraduate schools in New York state. Tuition aid is renewable through doctoral programs. Contact the address above for more information.

New York State Higher Education Services Corporation (Vietnam Veteran Vocational-Technical Grants)
Amount: $250.00 to $500.00 per semester
Deadline: September 1
College Major: Vocational/Technical
Requirements: Scholarships are open to Vietnam Veterans who are New York residents and are enrolled at a recognized vocational and technical school in New York. Scholarships are renewable for four years. Write for complete details.

New York State Higher Education Services Corporation (Vietnam Veterans College Tuition Grants)
Amount: $1000.00 Full time; $500.00 Part time
Deadline: May 1
College Major: All Majors
Requirements: Grants are open to Vietnam Veterans who served in Indochina between January 1, 1963 and May 7, 1975, are New York residents and are enrolled at specific institutions in New York state. Scholarships are renewable for up to four years. Write for more information.

North Carolina
North Carolina Association of Educators (Undergraduate Scholarships)

MLK Scholarship Fund
P.O. Box 27347
Raleigh, NC 27611
Amount: Varies
Deadline: February 1
College Major: Education
Requirements: Scholarships are open to undergraduate seniors who are enrolled at any recognized college or university in North Carolina. Applicant must be a U.S. citizen or legal resident. Recipients are required to teach for a minimum of two year in North Carolina after the completion for their degree. Please write for application and more information.

North Dakota

North Dakota Student Financial Assistance Agency (Student Incentive Grant Program)
10th Floor; Capitol Building
600 East Boulevard
Bismark, ND 58505-0230
Amount: $600.00
Deadline: April 15
College Major: All Majors
Requirements: Grants are available to North Dakota resident high school graduates who are full time students at a North Dakota college or university. Write for more information.

Ohio

Ohio Board of Regents (Graduate/Professional Fellowship)
30 East Broad Street Rm 3600
Columbus, OH 43266
Amount: $3500.00
Deadline: March 1
College Major: All Majors
Requirements: Fellowships are available to Ohio resident graduate students who are attending an accredited college or university. Applicants must have taken a graduate school exam. Write for more information.

Ohio Board of Regents (Ohio Academic Scholarship Program)
Amount: $1000.00
Deadline: February 23
College Major: All Majors
Requirements: Seniors at eligible Ohio high schools, Ohio residents and those enrolled as full time undergraduate students in eligible Ohio colleges or universities (or who plan to enroll). Applicants must be US citizens. Approximately 1000 scholarships are allocated each year. Scholarships are automatically renewable as long as the recipients maintain a satisfactory g.p.a. Please write for more information.

Ohio Board of Regents (Ohio Instructional Grants)
Amount: $174.00 to $1092.00 (public institutions); $435.00 to $2724.00 (private institutions)
Deadline: August 21
College Major: All Majors
Requirements: Students who are U.S. citizens, residents of Ohio and enrolled full time in academic institutions in Ohio are eligible to apply. Requirements include good academic standing and proven financial need. Approximately 90000 renewable grants are awarded annually. Please write for more information.

Ohio Board of Regents (Ohio Student Choice Grant)
Amount: $700.00
Deadline: Determined by institution
College Major: All Majors
Requirements: Applicants must be U.S. citizens, Ohio residents and enrolled full time in undergraduate study in an eligible private non-profit college or university in Ohio. Approximately 23000 renewable awards are given each year. Please write for more information.

Ohio Board of Regents (War Orphans Scholarships)
Amount: Full tuition at public schools; equivalent at private schools
Deadline: July 1
College Major: All Majors
Requirements: These scholarships are open to Ohio residents who are dependents of Veterans who served for 90+ days during conflict and are 60%+ disabled or deceased. Applicant must be 16 to 21 years of age and pursuing an associate's or bachelor's degree. Please write for more information.

Ohio (Southwestern) Council for Higher Education (SOCHE/Frigidaire Scholarship)
2900 Acosta Street, Suite 141
Dayton, OH 45420
Amount: $800.00 to $1600.00
Deadline: May 1
College Major: All Majors
Requirements: Scholarships are available to the children, spouses or employees of any General Motors division in Montgomery County, OH. Applicant must be accepted or enrolled in college and have at least a 3.0 g.p.a. (4.0 scale). Please write for more information.

Ohio (Southwestern) Council for Higher Education (SOCHE/PGA Scholarship)
Amount: Varies
Deadline: Varies
College Major: All Majors
Requirements: Scholarships are available to minority students who have enrolled in one of the Council institutions. Selection is based on financial need. Please write for more information.

Ohio Student Aid Commission (Student Loan Program)
309 South 4th Street
Columbus, OH 43215
Amount: Varies
Deadline: None specified
College Major: All Majors
Requirements: Loans are available to US citizens or legal residents who are Ohio residents, attending an Ohio institution or find a Ohio lender. Applicants must have at least a 2.0 g.p.a. and demonstrate financial need. Loans are renewable. Write for more information.

Ohio Student Aid Commission (Paul Douglas Teacher Scholarship)
Amount: $5000.00 to $20000.00
Deadline: None specified
College Major: Education
Requirements: Applicants must be college freshmen attending an Ohio school and are US citizens, and are Ohio residents with a high school education or equivalent. Selections are based on academics and a good student loan record. The funds are automatically renewed each year if eligibility is maintained. Write for more information.

Oklahoma

Oklahoma State Regents for Higher Education (Oklahoma Tuition Aid Grant Program)
500 Education Building
State Capitol Complex
Oklahoma City, OK 73105
Amount: $2625.00 to $4000.00
Deadline: April 30
College Major: All Majors
Requirements: Grants are available to residents of Oklahoma who are attending specified public or private colleges or universities within Oklahoma. Applicants must show financial need. Please write for more information.

Oregon

Oregon State Scholarship Commission (Alan B Holmes Memorial Scholarship)
1500 Valley River Drive, Suite 100
Eugene, OR 97401
Amount: Varies
Deadline: March 15
College Major: All Majors
Requirements: Scholarships are available to graduating seniors from Ashland, Butte Falls, Crater, Eagle Point, North Medford, South Medford, Phoenix, Prospect or Rogue River High Schools. Applicant must write an essay about how golf has contributed to the development of the applicant's life. Write for more information.

Oregon State Scholarship Commission (Alice Mellema Scholarship)
Amount: Varies
Deadline: March 15
College Major: All Majors
Requirements: Scholarships are available to graduating seniors of Sheridan High School. Write for more information.

Oregon State Scholarship Commission (Alpha Delta Kappa - Harriet Simmons Scholarship)
Amount: Varies
Deadline: March 15
College Major: Education
Requirements: Scholarships are open to students who are seniors majoring in education and plan to pursue a teaching certificate. Please write for application and more information.

Oregon State Scholarship Commission (Anna Jones Scholarship)
Amount: Varies
Deadline: March 15
College Major: All Majors
Requirements: Scholarships are available to residents of Lake County, Oregon who graduated from Paisley public schools. Applicants must attend an Oregon college or university. Write for more information.

Oregon State Scholarship Commission (Barbers and Hairdressers Grant)
Amount: $300.00 to $1500.00
Deadline: December 1
College Major: Cosmetology/ Barbering
Requirements: Funds are available to students currently attending a recognized school of cosmetology in the state. Applicants must be residents of Oregon in order to be eligible. Write to for more information.

Oregon State Scholarship Commission (Bertha B Singer Nurses Scholarship)
Amount: $300.00 to $1500.00
Deadline: Varies
College Major: Nursing
Requirements: Scholarships are open to graduates of Oregon high schools or residents of Oregon of at least one year. Applicant must be accepted full time in an accredited nursing program in Oregon and have a minimum g.p.a. of 3.0. Please write for application and more information.

Oregon State Scholarship Commission (Burns Lions Club)
Amount: Varies
Deadline: March 15
College Major: All Majors
Requirements: Scholarships are available to graduating seniors from Burns or Crane high schools in Oregon. Write for more information.

Oregon State Scholarship Commission (Carolyn Davies Memorial Scholarship)
Amount: Varies
Deadline: March 15
College Major: All Majors
Requirements: Scholarships are available to graduating seniors from Burns or Crane High Schools in Oregon. Write for more information.

Oregon State Scholarship Commission (Chuck Caffall Memorial Scholarship)
Amount: Varies
Deadline: March 15
College Major: Forestry/International Business
Requirements: Scholarships are available to graduating high school seniors who are studying one of the above majors and attend Newberg High School in Oregon. Write for more information.

Oregon State Scholarship Commission (Dan Konnie Scholarship)
Amount: Varies
Deadline: March 15
College Major: All Majors
Requirements: Scholarships are available to graduating high school seniors from Elmira, Crow or Triangle Lake High Schools. Must plan to attend an Oregon college or university. Write for more information.

Oregon State Scholarship Commission (Doane Education Trust Fund)
Amount: Varies
Deadline: March 15
College Major: All Majors
Requirements: Scholarships are available to residents of Wasco County, Oregon. Write for more information.

Oregon State Scholarship Commission (Fernridge Rural Fire District Scholarship)
Amount: Varies
Deadline: March 15
College Major: All Majors
Requirements: Scholarships are available to high school graduates of Elmira High School in Oregon who intend to enroll in an Oregon college or university. Write for more information.

Oregon State Scholarship Commission (Flora M Von Der Ahe)
Amount: $200.00 to $750.00

Deadline: Varies
College Major: All Majors
Requirements: Scholarships are open to students who graduated from high schools in Umatilla County, Oregon. Applicant must be enrolled full time in a recognized college, university or technical school in Oregon and have a 2.5 g.p.a.. Please write for application and more information.

Oregon State Scholarship Commission (Harland Cravat/Gray Johnson Scholarship)
Amount: Varies
Deadline: March 15
College Major: All Majors
Requirements: Scholarships are available to graduating high school seniors from Milwaukie High School in Oregon. Write for more information.

Oregon State Scholarship Commission (International Union of Operating Engineers Local 701)
Amount: Varies
Deadline: March 15
College Major: All Majors
Requirements: Scholarships are open to the children of union members in good standing. Please write for application and more information.

Oregon State Scholarship Commission (Jerome B Steinbach Scholarship)
Amount: Varies
Deadline: Varies
College Major: All Majors
Requirements: Scholarships are open to undergraduate students who are residents of Oregon. Applicants must have at least 3.25 g.p.a. and must be U.S. citizens by birth. Selection is based on academic achievement and financial need. Please write for application and more information.

Oregon State Scholarship Commission (John Paul Brown Loan Program)
Amount: Varies
Deadline: March 15
College Major: All Majors
Requirements: Scholarships are available to graduates of West Linn High School in Oregon. Applicants must attend an Oregon college. Write for more information.

Oregon State Scholarship Commission (KGON Scholarship)
Amount: Varies
Deadline: March 15
College Major: Broadcasting/Journalism
Requirements: Scholarships are available to residents of Washington, Multnomah, Clackamas, Clark or Yamhill counties who are interested in the above major. Write for more information.

Oregon State Scholarship Commission (Maria Jackson/General George A White Scholarship)
Amount: Varies
Deadline: March 15
College Major: All Majors
Requirements: Scholarships are available to Oregon residents who have served in the U.S. Armed Forces. Must have a 3.5 g.p.a. and attend an Oregon college. Write for more information.

Oregon State Scholarship Commission (Marie Mahoney Egan Scholarship)
Amount: Varies
Deadline: March 15

College Major: All Majors
Requirements: Scholarships are available to Lake County High School graduates who are residents of Lake County, Oregon. Write for more information.

Oregon State Scholarship Commission (Mertie & Harley Stevens Memorial Fund)
Amount: $250.00 to $2500.00
Deadline: Varies
College Major: All Majors
Requirements: Scholarships are open to students who are residents of Oregon and have graduated from a high school in Clakamas County in Oregon. Applicant must be entering their first year of undergraduate study and have a g.p.a. of 3.5. Please write for application and more information.

Oregon State Scholarship Commission (Multnomah County Deputy Sheriffs Association)
Amount: Varies
Deadline: March 15
College Major: Law Enforcement
Requirements: Scholarships are available to graduating high school seniors pursuing an education in the above field. Must have graduated from Barlow, Centennial, Corbett, David Douglas, Gresham, Parkrose, or Reynolds high schools. Write for more information.

Oregon State Scholarship Commission (Oregon Cash Awards; Oregon Need Grants)
Amount: Up to $732.00; $1500.00 (need grants)
Deadline: June 1
College Major: All Majors
Requirements: US citizens or legal residents of Oregon attending a two or four year non-profit school in Oregon for undergraduate study may apply. Applicants must demonstrate financial need. Need grant applicants need not take the SAT or ACT. Approximately 22,000 renewable awards and grants are given each year. Please write for more information.

Oregon State Scholarship Commission (Paul Douglas Memorial Teacher Scholarship)
Amount: Varies
Deadline: March 15
College Major: Education
Requirements: Scholarships are available to students who are in the top 10% of their high school class who are interested in a teaching career. Write for more information.

Oregon State Scholarship Commission (Peter Connacher Scholarship)
Amount: Varies
Deadline: March 15
College Major: All Majors
Requirements: Scholarships are available to former American POWs and their descendants. Write for more information.

Oregon State Scholarship Commission (Professional Land Surveyors of Oregon)
Amount: Varies
Deadline: March 15
College Major: Surveying
Requirements: Scholarships are open to students who are in their junior of a program leading to a career in land surveying. Please write for application and more information.

Oregon State Scholarship Commission (Richard John Cowan Memorial Scholarship)
Amount: Varies
Deadline: March 15

College Major: All Majors
Requirements: Scholarships are available to graduating high school seniors from Burns or Crane High Schools in Oregon. Write for more information.

Oregon State Scholarship Commission (Robert Byrd Scholarship)
Amount: Varies
Deadline: March 15
College Major: All Majors
Requirements: Scholarships are available to Oregon high school seniors with a minimum g.p.a. of 3.85 and 1150 SAT scores. Write for more information.

Oregon State Scholarship Commission (Scholarships for Children of Deceased or Disabled Oregon Peace Officers)
Amount: Varies
Deadline: Varies
College Major: All Majors
Requirements: Scholarships are open to the children of deceased or disabled Oregon Peace Officers. Awards are for undergraduate study only. Please write for application and more information.

Oregon State Scholarship Commission (Westside Professional & Business Associates)
Amount: Varies
Deadline: March 15
College Major: Business
Requirements: Scholarships are open to students who are residents of Washington, Multomah or Clakamas Counties. Applicant must be in their sophomore year in a business program. Please write for application and more information.

Pennsylvania
Pennsylvania Higher Education Assistance Agency (Grants for POW/MIA Dependents)
660 Boas Street Townhouse
Harrisburg, PA 17102
Amount: 80% of tuition and fees
Deadline: May 1
College Major: All Majors
Requirements: Dependents of parents who were members of the Armed Services serving after January 31, 1955 and are POWs or MIAs qualify for these grants. Applicants must also be residents of Pennsylvania. Awards are for undergraduate study only and are renewable. Write for more information.

Pennsylvania Higher Education Assistance Agency (Paul Douglas Teacher Scholarship Program)
Town House
Harrisburg, PA 17102
Amount: $5000.00
Deadline: May 1
College Major: Education
Requirements: Scholarships are available to Pennsylvania residents of at least one year. Applicant must be a graduating high school senior or an undergraduate student and a U.S. citizen or legal resident. Awards can be used at any accredited college or university in Pennsylvania. Applicant must also be committed to striving for a career as a teacher at the elementary and secondary school level. Write for more information.

Pennsylvania Higher Education Assistance Agency (PHEAA Alternative Loan)
P.O. Box 8114

Harrisburg, PA 17105-8114
Amount: Up to $10000.00
Deadline: None
College Major: All Majors
Requirements: Loans are available to Pennsylvania resident college students. Co-signer is required. Credit check is mandatory. Write for more information.

Pennsylvania Higher Education Assistance Agency (Robert C. Byrd Honors Scholarship)
Amount: $1500.00
Deadline: May 1
College Major: All Majors
Requirements: Scholarships are available to Pennsylvania resident high school graduates who are accepted in an accredited college or university. Applicants must have a 3.5 g.p.a., an 1100 SAT score, a 27 ACT score, or be in the upper 5% of their class. Applicants must fulfill two of the above requirements. Write for more information.

Pennsylvania Higher Education Assistance Agency (Scholars in Education Award)
Amount: $1500.00 to $5000.00
Deadline: May 1
College Major: Education
Requirements: Scholarships are available to Pennsylvania resident teaching students who are interested in teaching math or science. Applicants must be attending a Pennsylvania school, have a SAT math score of 550, have a 3.0 g.p.a., and are in the upper 20% of their class. Write for more information.

Rhode Island
Rhode Island Higher Education Assistance Authority (Loan Program)
560 Jefferson Boulevard
Warwick, RI 02886
Amount: Up to $4000.00 for undergraduates; up to $7500.00 for graduates
Deadline: None specified
College Major: All Majors
Requirements: Loans are available to undergraduate or graduate students attending an accredited degree granting institution in the state of Rhode Island. Applicants are not required to be residents, but must show need. Write to the above address for more information.

Rhode Island Higher Education Assistance Authority (Paul Douglas Teacher Scholarship)
Amount: $5000.00
Deadline: March 1
College Major: Education
Requirements: Rhode Island residents who have high academic records are qualified for these scholarships. Applicants must plan to attend a Rhode Island college or university. Awards are renewable upon proof of academic progress and proof that student is a full time Education major. Write to the Principal Program Analyst for more information.

Rhode Island Higher Education Assistance Authority (Undergraduate Grant and Scholarship Program)
Amount: $250.00 to $2000.00
Deadline: March 1
College Major: All Majors
Requirements: Scholarships are open to undergraduate students who are attending or planning to attend an accredited degree granting institution in Rhode Island, and who are residents of the state. Write to the above address for more information.

South Carolina

South Carolina Student Loan Corporation
P.O. Box 21487
Columbia, SC 29221
Amount: Varies
Deadline: Varies
College Major: All Majors
Requirements: Loans are available to students who need assistance financing their education. Applicants must be attending an accredited degree granting institution and pursuing either an undergraduate or graduate degree. Write for more information.

South Carolina Tuition Grants Committee (Higher Education Tuition Grants Program)
411 Keenan Building
P.O. Box 12159
Columbia SC 29211
Amount: Up to $2890.00
Deadline: June 30
College Major: All Majors
Requirements: Grants are available to students who are attending an accredited private college or university in South Carolina. Applicants must be residents of the state at the time of applying. There are 7500 renewable grants awarded every year which are renewable. Write for more information.

South Dakota

South Dakota Board of Regents (South Dakota State Veterans Tuition Waiver Program)
207 East Capitol Avenue
Pierre, SD 57501
Amount: Tuition
Deadline: None
College Major: All Majors
Requirements: This program is open to veterans who reside in the state of South Dakota. To be eligible, these veterans must have used all of their entitled benefits. Awards must be used to obtain a bachelors degree at an accredited college or university in the US. Write for more information.

South Dakota Department of Education and Cultural Affairs (Paul Douglas Teacher Scholarship)
700 Governors Drive
Pierre, SD 57501
Amount: $5000.00
Deadline: May 1
College Major: Education
Requirements: Scholarships are available to South Dakota resident college students pursuing a career in teaching. Must have graduated in the upper 10% of your high school class. Write for more information.

South Dakota Department of Education and Cultural Affairs (Robert C. Byrd Honors Scholarship)
Amount: $1500.00
Deadline: May 1
College Major: All Majors
Requirements: Scholarships are available to South Dakota resident college students who are enrolled in a South Dakota college or university. Must be a US citizen. Write for more information.

South Dakota Department of Education and Cultural Affairs (State Student Incentive Grant)
Amount: $100.00 to $600.00

Deadline: None specified
College Major: All Majors
Requirements: Funds are available to students who are attending an accredited degree granting institution in the state of South Dakota. Applicants must be residents at the time of applying for these renewable awards. Write to for more information.

South Dakota Department of Education and Cultural Affairs (Superior Scholar Program)
Amount: $1500.00
Deadline: June 1
College Major: All Majors
Requirements: Funds are available to students who are attending an accredited degree granting institution in the state of South Dakota. Applicants must be residents and National Merit Scholars as determined by the PSAT test. Write to for more information.

South Dakota Department of Education and Cultural Affairs (Tuition Equalization Grant)
Amount: $100.00 to $300.00
Deadline: April 1
College Major: All Majors
Requirements: Funds are available to students who are attending an accredited degree granting undergraduate or private institution in the state of South Dakota. Applicants must be residents at the time of applying for these renewable awards. Write to for more information.

Tennessee
Tennessee State Assistance Corporation (Paul Douglas Teacher Scholarship)
Pkwy Towers, Suite 1950
404 James Robertson Parkway
Nashville, TN 37219
Amount: Up to $5000.00
Deadline: March 1
College Major: Education
Requirements: Students are eligible for these funds if they are undergraduate freshmen who have graduated from a Tennessee high school in the top tenth of their class, have at least a 3.0 g.p.a. and are willing to sign an intent to teach after their schooling. Recipients must teach two years for each year the funds are used. The awards are renewable. Write to the Program Administrator for more information.

Tennessee State Assistance Corporation (Student Assistance Scholarships)
Amount: $1194.00
Deadline: August 1
College Major: All Majors
Requirements: Funds are available to residents of Tennessee who are pursuing a post secondary education at an accredited degree granting institution. Write for more information.

Tennessee State Assistance Corporation (Tennessee Community College Education Recruitment Scholarship)
Amount: $2000.00
Deadline: None
College Major: Education
Requirements: Scholarships are offered to Tennessee resident minority community college students. Applicants must be full time students pursuing the above major and be US citizens. Write for more information.

Tennessee State Assistance Corporation (Tennessee Dependent Children Scholarship)
Amount: Tuition

Deadline: July 15
College Major: All Majors
Requirements: Scholarships are offered to Tennessee residents who are children of deceased or permanently and totally disabled police officers, firemen or emergency medical service technicians from Tennessee. Write for more information.

Tennessee State Assistance Corporation (Tennessee Student Assistance Award)
Amount: Varies
Deadline: January 1 to August 1
College Major: All Majors
Requirements: Scholarships are offered to Tennessee resident undergraduate college students who are enrolled in a Tennessee college or university. Applicant must be a U.S. citizen. Write for more information.

Tennessee State Assistance Corporation (Tennessee Teacher Loan for Disadvantaged Areas)
Amount: Tuition
Deadline: May 15
College Major: Education
Requirements: Loans are available to Tennessee resident college students pursuing a career in teaching. Applicants must be enrolled in a Tennessee college or university. Write for more information.

Tennessee State Assistance Corporation (Tennessee Teacher Loan/Scholarship)
Amount: Tuition
Deadline: May 15
College Major: Education
Requirements: Scholarships are available to Tennessee resident college students majoring in the above field of study. Applicants must be attending a Tennessee public college or university. Write for more information.

Tennessee State Assistance Corporation (Tennessee Teaching Fellowships)
Amount: Up to $20000.00
Deadline: None
College Major: Education
Requirements: Fellowships are available to Tennessee resident minority college freshman who are pursuing the above major. Applicants must have a 3.5 g.p.a. in high school. Write for more information.

Texas
Texas Higher Education Coordinating Board (Hinson-Hazlewood College Student Loan)
P.O. Box 12788
Capitol Station
Austin, TX 78711
Amount: Varies
Deadline: None
College Major: All Majors
Requirements: Loans are available to Texas resident college students. Write for more information.

Texas Higher Education Coordinating Board (Texas College Access Loan)
Amount: Up to $25000.00
Deadline: None
College Major: All Majors

Requirements: Loans are available to Texas resident college students who are attending a Texas college full time. Write for more information.

Texas Higher Education Coordinating Board (Texas Health Education Assistance Loan)
Amount: Up to $20000.00
Deadline: None
College Major: Medicine/Osteopathy/Dentistry/Optometry/Podiatry/Veterinary Medicine/Pharmacy/Public Health/Chiropractic/Health Administration/Clinical Psychology
Requirements: Scholarships are available to doctoral students who are studying in one of the above fields of study and can prove financial need. Write for more information.

Texas Higher Education Coordinating Board (Texas Health Professions Student Loan)
Amount: $2500.00
Deadline: None
College Major: Medicine/Osteopathy
Requirements: Loans are available to doctoral students who are studying in one of the above fields of study. Write for more information.

Texas Higher Education Coordinating Board (Texas Nursing Student Loans and Scholarships)
Amount: Up to $13000.00
Deadline: None
College Major: Nursing
Requirements: Loans and scholarships are available to Texas resident college nursing students who are seeking financial aid. Write for more information.

Texas Higher Education Coordinating Board (Texas Public Educational Grant)
Amount: Varies
Deadline: None
College Major: All Majors
Requirements: Grants are available to college students who are seeking financial aid at a public Texas college or university. Write for more information.

Texas Higher Education Coordinating Board (Texas State Scholarship Program for Ethnic Recruitment)
Amount: $500.00 to $1000.00
Deadline: None
College Major: All Majors
Requirements: Scholarships are available to Texas resident minority students who are entering their first year in a Texas college or university on a full time basis. In order to be eligible you must have an 800 SAT score or 18 ACT score. Write for more information.

Texas Higher Education Coordinating Board (Texas State Student Incentive Grant for Students at Public Institutions)
Amount: Up to $1250.00
Deadline: None
College Major: All Majors
Requirements: Grants are available to college students who are attending a Texas public college or university. Write for more information.

Texas Higher Education Coordinating Board (Texas Tuition Equalization Grant)
Amount: Up to $1900.00
Deadline: None
College Major: All Majors

Requirements: Grants are available to Texas resident college students who are attending an independent college or university in Texas. Theology or religion degree majors are not eligible. Write for more information.

Utah

Utah Board of Regents (Student Incentive Grants; Educationally Disadvantaged Fund)
355 West North Temple 3 Triad, Suite 550
Salt Lake City, UT 84180
Amount: Varies
Deadline: None Specified
College Major: All Majors
Requirements: There are approximately 2000 awards given each year to Utah residents attending eligible Utah schools who are also US citizens or legal residents. These awards are designed to make incentive grants available to students in financial need. Write to the Utah institution you are interested in attending for more information.

Vermont

Vermont Student Assistance Corporation (Incentive Grants)
Champlain Mill; P.O. Box 2000
Winooski, VT 05404
Amount: $300.00 to $5100.00
Deadline: March 1
College Major: All Majors
Requirements: There are approximately 8000 grants awarded each year to Vermont residents who are high school graduates (or GED equivalent) planning to attend an approved undergraduate college or university. Applicants must show financial need and prove U.S. citizenship or legal residency. Students may already be enrolled in school. Write for more information.

Vermont Student Assistance Corporation (Non Degree Student Grant Program)
Amount: $325.00
Deadline: Varies
College Major: All Majors
Requirements: Grants are open to Vermont residents who are not enrolled in high school but enrolled in a non degree course that will improve employability or encourage further study. Selection is based on financial need. Please write for application and more information.

Virgin Islands

Virgin Islands Board of Education (Exceptional Children Scholarship)
P.O. Box 11900
St Thomas, VI 00801
Amount: $2000.00
Deadline: March 31
College Major: All Majors
Requirements: These scholarships are open to true residents of the Virgin Islands suffering from physical, mental, or emotional handicaps. Applicants must demonstrate ability to learn and the need for educational training beyond what is available in the Virgin Islands. Write for complete information.

Virgin Islands Board of Education (Music Scholarship)
Amount: $2000.00
Deadline: March 31
College Major: Music

Requirements: Scholarships are open to residents of the Virgin Islands who are enrolled in music program at a recognized college or university. Recipient must maintain a 2.0 average (4.0 scale) for the duration of the grant. Write for complete details.

Virgin Islands Board of Education (Nursing and other Health Scholarships)
Amount: Up to $1800.00
Deadline: March 31
College Major: Nursing/Medicine
Requirements: Scholarships are available to residents of the Virgin Islands who are admitted to a recognized school of nursing or a school that offers courses in a health related field. Recipients must maintain a 'C' average to continue receiving the awards. Write for complete details.

Virgin Islands Board of Education (Territorial Scholarship Grants)
Amount: $1000.00 to $3000.00
Deadline: March 31
College Major: All Majors
Requirements: These grants are open to native residents of the Virgin Islands who are enrolled in a recognized college or university with a cumulative g.p.a. of at least a 2.0. There are approximately 400 awards given each year which are renewable as long as satisfactory grades are maintained. Loans are also available. Write for more information.

Virginia
Virginia State Council of Higher Education (College Scholarship Assistance Program)
James Monroe Building
101 North 14th Street
Richmond, VA 23219
Amount: $400.00 to $2000.00
Deadline: Varies
College Major: All Majors
Requirements: This program is offered to Virginia residents who are undergraduates at specific Virginia institutes of higher education. Contact the above address for information.

Virginia State Council of Higher Education (Eastern Shore Tuition Assistance Program)
Amount: Varies
Deadline: Open
College Major: All Majors
Requirements: This program is available to residents of Northampton or Accomack Counties who enrolled as commuting juniors or seniors at Salisbury State College or the University of Maryland-Eastern Shore. Bachelor's or higher degree holders & religion majors are not eligible. Write for more information.

Virginia State Council of Higher Education (Lee-Jackson Foundation Scholarship)
Amount: Varies
Deadline: February 3
College Major: All Majors
Requirements: These scholarships were created to continue the memory of the character and virtues of Generals Robert E. Lee and Thomas "Stonewall" Jackson. Awards are given to seniors and juniors enrolled in public or private Virginia high schools. Basis for selection is based on an essay contest which examine and demonstrate the virtues of Lee & Jackson. Applications are available from secondary principals every September or write to the above address.

Virginia State Council of Higher Education (National Science Scholars Program)
Amount: Varies

Deadline: October 15
College Major: Engineering/Mathematics/Computer Science/Physics
Requirements: Scholarships are available to students that have demonstrated exceptional academic achievement in science related courses during their secondary education. Awards are renewable for up to four years. Applications are available from a secondary school principal in mid-September or write to the council for more information.

Virginia State Council of Higher Education (Paul Douglas Teacher Scholarship Program)
Amount: $5000.00
Deadline: Varies
College Major: Education
Requirements: Scholarships are open to students registered in a teacher certification program. Applicant must have graduated in the top 10% of their class and a U.S. citizen or legal resident. Scholarships are to be repaid if the obligation of teaching in a critical shortage area for each year aid is received is not fulfilled. Please write application and more information.

Virginia State Council of Higher Education (Tuition Assistance Grant Program)
Amount: $1500.00
Deadline: June 1
College Major: All Majors
Requirements: Renewable grants are available to Virginia residents who are full time undergraduate, graduate or professional students at eligible private colleges and universities in Virginia. Available regardless of need. Write for complete information.

Virginia State Council of Higher Education (Undergraduate Student Financial Assistance Program)
Amount: Varies
Deadline: Open
College Major: All Majors
Requirements: These grants are available to African-American students on a need basis to assist them in attending Virginia state-supported schools. Contact your school's financial aid office for additional information.

Virginia State Council of Higher Education (Virginia Scholars Program)
Amount: $3000.00
Deadline: December 15, May 15
College Major: All Majors
Requirements: This program is for Virginia residents. The grant awards are merit based for outstanding high school seniors or graduates of a public two year college who plan to enroll as full time undergraduates at a four year Virginia college or university. Applicants must be nominated by their high school or their two year college. The grants are renewable up to three years. Write for more information.

Virginia State Council of Higher Education (Virginia Transfer Grant Program)
Amount: Tuition + Fees
Deadline: Varies
College Major: All Majors
Requirements: Virginia residents of minority status are eligible for these awards to be used at a four year public Virginia school. Write for more information.

Virginia State Council on Higher Education (Soil Scientists Program)
Amount: Tuition + Fees
Deadline: Varies
College Major: Soil Science

Requirements: Awards are available to students interested in pursuing a career in soil science at Virginia Tech. Recipients must agree to work one year in the field for each year the scholarship is received. For more information call (703) 231-9778.

Virginia State Council on Higher Education (State Cadetships)
Amount: Tuition + Fees
Deadline: Varies
College Major: All Majors
Requirements: Funds are available to state cadets of Virginia who are interested in attending the Virginia Military Institute. Award covers tuition, fees, and room and board. For more information, call (703) 464-7208.

Virginia State Council on Higher Education (State Law Enforcement Officers Educational Program)
Amount: Tuition
Deadline: Varies
College Major: Law Enforcement
Requirements: Funds are available to law enforcement officers who are Virginia residents and are planning on attending, or currently enrolled in an institute of higher education. The state provides tuition reimbursement to recipients. Call the Criminal Justice Services Training Division at (804) 786-7801 for more information.

Virginia State Council on Higher Education (Teaching Scholarship Loan Program)
Amount: $2000.00
Deadline: May 15
College Major: Education
Requirements: Funds are available to Virginia state residents who are enrolled in their final two years of an accredited teacher preparation program. Recipients must agree to work in the state in an area where there is a shortage of teachers. Write to the above address for more information.

Washington

Washington State Higher Education Coordinating Board (Washington Rural Physician, Pharmacist, and Midwife)
P.O. Box 43430
Olympia, WA 98504
Amount: $4000.00 to $15000.00
Deadline: None
College Major: Medicine/Pharmacy/Midwives
Requirements: Scholarships are available to Washington resident college students who are involved in one of the above fields of study. Recipients must serve in rural areas where there are shortages of professional services. Write for more information.

Washington State Higher Education Coordinating Board (American Indian Endowed Scholarship)
Amount: Varies
Deadline: Open
College Major: All Majors
Requirements: Scholarships are available to Native Americans who are Washington State residents and show financial need. Write to the board to receive more information.

Washington State Higher Education Coordinating Board (Christa McAuliffe Award for Excellence)
Amount: Varies
Deadline: Open

College Major: Education
Requirements: This award is available to teachers, principals, and school administrators in recognition of outstanding contributions to education. Applicants must be Washington State teachers and the funds are to be used for 45 quarter or 30 semester credits of coursework. Write to the board for more information.

Washington State Higher Education Coordinating Board (Paul Fowler Scholarship)
Amount: $2830.00
Deadline: Open
College Major: All Majors
Requirements: This is a privately-funded scholarship for outstanding Washington Scholars. Applicants must "have demonstrated outstanding ability and willingness to work for an education." Write to the board for additional information.

Washington State Higher Education Coordinating Board (Professional Student Exchange Program)
Amount: $7100.00
Deadline: Open
College Major: Optometry
Requirements: This program provides state money to optometry students who are residents of Washington State and enrolled out of state. Nineteen awards are available. Write for additional information.

Washington State Higher Education Coordinating Board (Washington Aid to Blind Students)
Amount: $200.00 to $300.00
Deadline: August 15
College Major: All Majors
Requirements: Scholarships are available to blind college students who are residents of Washington. Applicants must attend a Washington college or university. Write for more information.

Washington State Higher Education Coordinating Board (Washington Educational Opportunity Grant)
Amount: $2500.00
Deadline: None
College Major: All Majors
Requirements: Grants are available to Washington residents with an Associate of Arts degree who are pursuing further education. Write for information.

Washington State Higher Education Coordinating Board (Washington Future Teacher Conditional Scholarship)
Amount: Up to $3000.00
Deadline: April 15
College Major: Education
Requirements: Scholarships are available to students who are Washington residents and are pursuing a degree in teaching. Awards are renewable for up to five years and require a ten-year Washington public school teaching commitment. Write for information.

Washington State Higher Education Coordinating Board (Washington Health Professional Loan Repayment)
Amount: Up to $15000.00
Deadline: None
College Major: Health Sciences
Requirements: Loans are available to Washington residents who are health professionals seeking to become licensed in Washington State. Write for more information.

Washington State Higher Education Coordinating Board (Washington Scholars)
Amount: Four Year Tuition
Deadline: November
College Major: All Majors
Requirements: Scholarships are available to Washington resident high school seniors who rank academically in the top three in their respective legislative district. Scholarship goes toward tuition at a Washington public or private college. Write for information.

Washington State Higher Education Coordinating Board (WICHE Regional Graduate Exchange)
Amount: Varies
Deadline: Open
College Major: All Majors
Requirements: The Western Interstate Commission for Higher Education Student Exchange (WICHE) program for graduates allows Washington State residents to enroll in masters and doctorate programs not available in the state. There are 13 participating states with 125 programs at 35 graduate schools. Write to the board at the above address for more information.

Washington State Higher Education Coordination Board (Washington State Need Grant Program)
Amount: Varies
Deadline: August 1
College Major: All Majors
Requirements: This program is open to Washington state residents of at least one year. Awards can be used at any eligible undergraduate institution in Washington. Applicants must be U.S. citizens or legal residents. Selection is based on financial need. Write for more information.

Washington State Higher Education (Washington Nurses Conditional Scholarship)
Amount: Up to $3000.00
Deadline: None
College Major: Nursing
Requirements: Loans are available to Washington resident nursing students. Recipients must work for the state after graduation to pay for the loan. Write for more information.

West Virginia
West Virginia Higher Education Grant Program (Grants)
P.O. Box 4007
Charleston, WV 25364
Amount: $350.00 to $1968.00
Deadline: March 1
College Major: All Majors
Requirements: Grants are available to residents of West Virginia of at least one year. Applicant must be a high school graduate and enrolled in a full time undergraduate program at an eligible institution in West Virginia. Applicant must also have financial need and be making satisfactory academic progress. There are 4500 grants awarded per year which are renewable for up to eight semesters. Write for more information.

West Virginia Higher Education Grant Program (Paul Douglas Teacher Scholarship Program)
Amount: Varies
Deadline: Varies
College Major: All Majors
Requirements: Scholarships are open to students who are residents of West Virginia. Applicant must be at the top 10% of his or her class, enrolled at an accredited college or university pursuing a teaching

certificate. Recipients are obligated to work for two years for each year of assistance at areas where there are teacher shortages. Please write for application and more information.

West Virginia Higher Education Grant Program (Robert C. Byrd Scholarship Program)
Amount: Varies
Deadline: March 15
College Major: All Majors
Requirements: Scholarships are open to West Virginia residents who are high school graduates. Applicant must demonstrate excellent academic achievement and must have been accepted for enrolled in an accredited college or university. Please write for application and more information.

West Virginia Higher Education Grant Program (Underwood-Smith Teacher Scholarship Program)
Amount: Varies
Deadline: Varies
College Major: Education
Requirements: Scholarships are open to West Virginia residents who are undergraduate students with a minimum g.p.a. of 3.25 and graduated in the top 10% of their class or graduate students who will graduating in the top 10% of their class. Applicant must be enrolled in an accredited college or university in West Virginia pursuing his or her teaching certificate. Recipients are obligated to teach for two year in public school in West Virginia. Please write for application and more information.

Wisconsin
Wisconsin Higher Education Aid Board (Academic Scholarships)
P.O. Box 7885
Madison, WI 53707
Amount: $2100.00
Deadline: April 15
College Major: All Majors
Requirements: Scholarships are available to Wisconsin high school seniors who have the highest g.p.a. in their respective school. Please write for more information.

Wisconsin Higher Education Aid Board (Education Grants Program)
Amount: Up to $1800.00
Deadline: Varies
College Major: Vocational/Technical
Requirements: Grants are available to Wisconsin residents who are attending one of the following schools for at least half time: University of Wisconsin, Wisconsin State Vocational-Technical or Adult Education Programs. Applicants must in need of financial aid and must demonstrate scholastic excellence. Grants are renewable for up to ten semesters. Write for more information.

Wisconsin Higher Education Aid Board (Minority Teachers Loans)
Amount: Up to $5000.00
Deadline: None
College Major: Education
Requirements: Loans are available to Wisconsin minority junior or senior college students studying education. Applicants must be Wisconsin residents. Write for more information.

Wisconsin Higher Education Aid Board (Native American Student Grants)
Amount: Up to $2200.00
Deadline: None specified
College Major: All Majors

Requirements: Residents of Wisconsin with a quarter degree or more Native American blood or tribal or band certification (with an appropriate Native American agency) are eligible to apply. Applicants must prove financial need. Recipients must be accepted for enrollment in an eligible Wisconsin institution of higher education. Grants are renewable for up to five years and include graduate study. Please write to the above address for complete information.

Wisconsin Higher Education Aid Board (Nursing Student Stipend Loans)
Amount: Up to $2500.00 per year
Deadline: Varies
College Major: Nursing
Requirements: Funds are available to Wisconsin residents who are full time nursing students in a program that grants an associate degree, bachelors degree or VTAE students. Applicants may receive up to $5000.00 total and the loan may be forgiven if the student works in a Wisconsin hospital for a certain period of time. Write to the above address for more information.

Wisconsin Higher Education Aid Board (Paul Douglas Teacher Scholarship)
Amount: Up to $5000.00
Deadline: None
College Major: Education
Requirements: Scholarships are available to high school seniors who are ranked in the top 10% of their class and are pursuing a major in teacher education. Applicants must be Wisconsin residents. Write for information.

Wisconsin Higher Education Aid Board (Student Loans Program)
Amount: Varies
Deadline: None specified
College Major: All Majors
Requirements: Students are eligible for these loans if they are U.S. citizens or legal residents, and Wisconsin residents. Applicants must be enrolled in eligible schools half or full time, maintain a good academic record, and demonstrate financial need. Write for more information.

Wisconsin Higher Education Aid Board (Talent Incentive Program)
Amount: $1800.00
Deadline: None
College Major: All Majors
Requirements: Scholarships are available to minority college students with financial need. Write for application information.

Wisconsin Higher Education Aid Board (Tuition Grant Program)
Amount: Up to $2172.00
Deadline: None
College Major: All Majors
Requirements: There are approximately 7600 renewable grants available each year to Wisconsin residents enrolled in nonprofit accredited colleges, universities, and nursing schools in Wisconsin. The schools must charge higher tuition than the University of Wisconsin-Madison. Applicants must meet academic requirements. Write for more information.

Wisconsin Higher Education Aid Board (Visual and Hearing Impaired Grants)
Amount: $1800.00
Deadline: None
College Major: All Majors
Requirements: Grants are available to blind and deaf college students who are Wisconsin residents. Applicants must have financial need. Contact for more information.

Alternative Finance Programs

Student Financial Services

Alternative Ways to Pay for a College Education

Today many colleges and universities are developing alternative and innovative ways for students to meet the rising costs of higher education. Over 200 schools nationwide offer several different tuition payment plans so you can select the plan that best fits your financial situation. These options offer all students, whether or not they qualify for financial aid, a chance to save some money during the course of their college education. The universities also benefit from these payment plans, because they can invest and earn interest on prepaid tuition. This is money they would eventually have, but are getting early through these programs.

These new programs are coming at a time when the cost of post-secondary education is increasing an average of five to ten percent each year. The following money-saving options provide the means to curb this tuition increase and enjoy college life without the continued burden of financial worries. From prepaying your tuition, to programs that accelerate the degree-earning process, you'll be able to find a money-saving plan that works for you.

TUITION PREPAYMENT PLANS

This type of program gives students and families the option of paying for their entire college career all at once or in the form of large installments, usually made once a year over a four-year period. You benefit by avoiding tuition increases. Most schools offer a single tuition rate as incentive for students and families to send payment before it is due. There are several prepayment programs available, and most schools have their own payment options.

Paying in Installments: Installments can be made monthly or yearly, with the benefit of a lock on the current tuition rate for paying early. Some schools even offer a sizable discount to students who pay an entire year's tuition at once.

One Payment: Paying for four years of school at one time can avoid tuition increases and save you hundreds, possibly thousands, of dollars over the course of college.

GUARANTEED TUITION PLAN

Several colleges and universities, usually expensive public or private schools, offer these types of plans to increase enrollment. Under this program, tuition is guaranteed, promising that the rate for the incoming student will not increase from the time of enrollment to graduation. This may also include boarding expenses. The main benefit of the guaranteed tuition plan is that it allows students and families to plan the entire amount of an education over a four-year period without worrying about increases in expenses.

ACCELERATED DEGREE COURSES

Students who can't afford the cost of a four-year or five-year education can enroll in accelerated programs that help students earn their baccalaureate degrees in less than four years. Most programs run for three intense years with classes year-round.

The Advanced Placement Exam-Earning Credit Before College: Most colleges and universities nationwide honor AP exams for credit. More than twenty different tests, in all types of areas ranging from foreign language to physics, are offered by the College Board. You take the exam in your senior year of high school and if you pass you are granted college credit for the course in which you took the test. Entering college with over fifteen AP credits could save you an entire quarter or semester's worth of tuition!

It's important to look for these types of programs when searching for schools. Most colleges and universities don't heavily advertise these options, so contact the Admissions or Financial Aid Office and ask if they offer any prepayment incentives or accelerated degree courses. Because college attendance is declining and tuition costs are rising, schools have begun to develop innovative ways to attract students. Some colleges offer tuition breaks to students whose parents are alumni. Schools will even match their tuition prices with those of lower-cost colleges. Each school has its own unique program, so make sure to ask. Don't be afraid to bargain with the school of your choice. Remember they want you to attend, too, and they may just make sure that you enroll.

Alternative Financing Programs

There are several ways to finance a college education, so don't be discouraged if the first few sources you researched weren't successful. In addition to the federal and state financial aid programs, there are many educational financing alternatives for students. Before deciding to investigate these alternative programs, make sure you have applied for all other financial aid available. Federal and state-funded programs are usually less expensive than programs that are privately funded by banks and lending institutions. However, if you can't qualify for the federal programs, or they don't cover the total amount of your educational costs, alternative financing programs are worth pursuing.

Following are some alternative financing programs.

ACADEMIC MANAGEMENT SERVICES (AMS)

AMS Monthly Budget Plan

This plan allows families to pay for college expenses with monthly payments. This is not a loan but rather a budgeting plan. Applicants can budget up to the total cost of their education, and an automatic life insurance policy is included with the plan. There are no interest charges, and the school determines the amount of the monthly payments and the length of the payback period. There is a $50 application fee.

AMS Extra & Academic Credit Line

This program is based on income and credit status. Applicants can be approved for a minimum credit line of $2,500 to a maximum of $25,000. The interest rate is variable and dependent on the prime rate (prime rate + four percent). There is an annual fee of $25 for loan borrowers, which is waived for the first year. The minimum monthly payment is two percent of the outstanding balance, but recipients can choose to pay the interest only, for two, four or six years. This program is a revolving credit line; therefore, funds become available as payments are made.

For more information and application forms, write to:

Academic Management Services
50 Vision Boulevard
East Providence, RI 02914

(800) 635-0120 or (800) 637-3060

BAY BANKS EDUCATION FINANCING PROGRAMS

Bay Bank Teri Loan

This is a privately-funded loan available to undergraduate students. Students who want to apply for this loan are required to have a co-signer to be eligible. The applicant can borrow up to the total cost of his or her education. The interest varies according to the prime rate (prime rate + two percent). The student must pay the interest while in school, and can defer payment of the principal until after graduation. Loan recipients have up to twenty-five years to repay the loan, depending on the amount borrowed, and payment begins forty-five days after graduation.

Bay Bank Pep Loan

This loan is also privately funded and is available to graduate students enrolled at least half-time in a graduate degree program. The interest rate is variable and dependent on the prime rate (prime rate + two percent). Recipients have up to twenty years to repay their loan, depending on the amount borrowed.

For more information and application forms, call: (800) 322-8374.

FAMILY EDUCATION FINANCING PLAN (SALLIE MAE)

Extra Credit

This program is based on the applicant's income. Students can borrow up to $25,000 per year. The interest is fixed at 7.25% and payments cannot be deferred. Recipients must begin payment as soon as funds are disbursed. The payback period ranges from ten to fifteen years, depending on the amount borrowed.

Extra Time

With this program, which is also based on the applicant's income, students can borrow a maximum of $25,000 a year. The interest rate varies, depending on the U.S. Treasury Bill (U.S. Treasury Bill + four and a half percent). Payments can be deferred only until after graduation. The payback period is ten years.

For more information and an application, write to:

Family Education Financing Operation
Loan Originations Center
P.O. Box 25526
Washington, DC 20007

(800) 831-LOAN

NELLIE MAE

Excel Loan Program

This loan program is based on income or credit status. Students who apply may be required to have a co-signer for the loan. Applicants can borrow a minimum of $2,000 a year. The interest rate varies, depending on the prime rate (prime rate + two percent monthly or + three percent yearly). Recipients must pay the interest while in school but payment of the principal can be deferred until after graduation. The payback period ranges from four to twenty years, depending on the amount borrowed.

Share Loan Program

This program is available to only thirty-two schools. It is an income-based program, where applicants can borrow up to the total cost of their education. Students who apply might be required to have a co-signer for the loan. The interest rate varies, depending on the prime rate (prime rate + two percent monthly or + three percent yearly). Recipients must pay the interest while in school but payment of the principal can be deferred until after graduation. The payback period ranges from four to twenty years, depending on the amount borrowed.

Gradshare Loan Program

This loan program is available to graduate students and is based on income and credit status. The interest rate varies, depending on the prime rate (prime rate + two percent monthly). Recipients must pay the interest while in school but payment of the principal can be deferred until after graduation. The payback period ranges from four to twenty years, depending on the amount borrowed.

For more information and application forms, write to:

Nellie Mae
Customer Service
50 Braintree Hill Park, Suite 300
Braintree, MA 02184
(800) 634-9308

EDUCATION RESOURCES INSTITUTE OF BOSTON-TERI

TERI Supplemental Loan

This loan program is available to undergraduate students or their parents. Eligibility is based on income and credit status, and students who apply may be required to have a co-signer. Applicants can borrow from $2,000 to $20,000. The interest rate is variable, depending on the prime rate (prime rate + two percent). Payment of the principal can be deferred for up to forty-five days after graduation. Recipients must pay interest while in school. The payback period is twenty-five years.

TERI Professional Education Plan (PEP)

This loan program is available to graduate students. Eligibility for this program is not based on need but on income and credit status. Applicants can borrow a maximum of $20,000 per year. The interest rate is variable, based on the prime rate. Deferment of payments is allowed. For more information and application forms, call: (800) 255-TERI.

EDUCATIONAL CREDIT CORPORATION

Education Credit Line (ECL)

This program is based on income and credit status. Applicants can borrow from $5,000 to $50,000. The interest rate varies, based on the prime rate (prime rate + two and a half percent). There is a $35 application fee.

Home Equity (Prime Solution)

This program is for parents who need help financing their children's college education. Homeowners with equity are eligible for this program. Applicants can borrow from $10,000 to $500,000. The interest rates range from 5 to 12%.

Graduate Loan/Career Starter Loan

This program is available to graduating college seniors or graduate students. Applicants can borrow from $1,000 to $10,000. The interest rate is variable, depending on the future earning potential of the borrower. There is a $25 application fee.

For more information and application forms, write to:

Educational Credit Corporation
140 Mayhew Way, Suite 100
Pleasant Hill, CA 94523
(800) 477-4977

Specialized Aid

Financial aid is available to anyone who is willing to look for it. Through funds from federal, state, or private organizations, millions of dollars in aid is offered to students based on ethnic background or personal make-up. Minorities, women, and physically challenged students are eligible to receive financial assistance not offered to the general student population. The purpose of offering extra assistance is to encourage members of these groups to continue their post-secondary education, and to increase the number of minorities, women, and physically challenged students currently attending a college or university.

These sources of aid also provide opportunities for students planning to pursue a career in certain professions. Education, health, and public service are just three of the areas which need more people to fill the employment positions available. In reaction to the lack of students entering these fields, federal and state-level governments have created incentive programs that offer scholarships and loans to anyone willing to earn a degree in one of these areas of study. The majority of the loans offered can be repaid or "forgiven" through a commitment to work as a teacher, public servant, or health professional for a certain period of time following graduation. This work may be located in rural areas of the United States with a shortage of people trained in these professions.

The following organizations will provide you with information about scholarships and loans offered by the federal government. Contact the financial aid office or counselor at your college or university for additional state and private aid programs.

Physically-Challenged Students

American Council for the Blind
1155 15th Street Northwest, Suite 720
Washington, DC 20005
(202) 467-5081

The Alexander Graham Bell
Association for the Deaf, Inc.
3417 Volta Place Northwest
Washington, DC 20007-2778
(202) 337-5220 (TDD and regular)

Minorities

The Bureau of Indian Affairs of
Higher Education
1849 C Street Northwest
MS 3512-MN Code 522
Washington, DC 20240
(202) 208-3710

Minority Access to Research Careers
Program (MARC)
NIGMS, Room 950
Westwood Building
Bethesda, MD 20892

National Action Council for
Minorities in Engineering
3 West 35th Street, 3rd Floor
New York, NY 10001
(212) 279-2626

National Advisory Council on Indian
Education

Mary Switzer Building, Room 4072
330 C Street Southwest
Washington, DC 20202-7556
(202) 205-8353

Youth and College Division
NAACP
1397 Fulton Street
Brooklyn, NY 11216
(718) 789-3043

Professions

HEALTH
Department of Health and Human
Services
200 Independence Avenue Southwest
Washington, DC 20201
(202) 619-0257

National League for Nursing
350 Hudson Street, 4th Floor
New York, NY 10014
(212) 989-9393

JOURNALISM
Journalism Scholarships Program
The Freedom Forum
1101 Wilson Boulevard
Arlington, VA 22209
(703) 528-0800

PUBLIC SERVICE
Harry S. Truman Scholarship
Foundation
712 Jackson Place Northwest
Washington, DC 20006
(202) 395-4831

TEACHING
Paul C. Douglas Teacher Scholarship
Contact your state agency for
information
page 56

Women
Business and Professional Women's
Foundation
2012 Massachusetts Avenue
Northwest
Washington, DC 20036
(202) 293-1200   *Sent for info 18DEC*

United Engineering Center
345 East 47th Street
New York, NY 10017
(212) 705-7000

Women's Sports Foundation
Eisenhower Park
East Meadow, NY 11554
(516) 542-4700

High School Students

Student Financial Services

High School Programs

Students who begin their search for financial aid information early will have a better idea of what type of aid they are eligible to receive and how they can obtain it. In fact, students who start looking early have more access to "free aid" than students who wait until the last minute to apply. The best way to maximize your chances for aid is to keep yourself open to everything. Your eligibility to receive grants, scholarships, and college admission is influenced by your activities, involvement, and academic achievement during high school. To increase your eligibility, you need to:

- Keep up your grades
- Become involved in extracurricular activities, athletics, clubs, or community service
- Run for a student body office
- Become involved in a youth group or a volunteer activity
- Work part-time
- Start looking into colleges and financial aid opportunities early

Participation in any of these activities will increase your eligibility for scholarships, grants, and loans, as well as make you aware of all the organizations that offer these types of awards to graduating high school seniors.

QUICK TIP: *Beginning your freshman year in high school, start a running list of your activities, sports, and any awards you may have received. Also include your job experience and a list of adults who can write letters of recommendation for your college admission and scholarship applications. This approach is much easier than having to recall everything you've done in the last three years.*

FINANCIAL AID INFORMATION SOURCES

Information on financial aid is widely available. You just need to know where and how to find it. The majority of students reduce the amount of aid they're eligible to receive by not searching enough, or looking in the wrong places. Billions of dollars in aid goes unclaimed every year because students don't realize that thousands of private companies, organizations, and state and federal agencies offer scholarships, grants, and loans. Here are a few places you might look:

- High school guidance counselors or career centers
- State agencies for higher education (see page 56)
- Colleges or universities you are interested in attending
- Your parents' companies or organizations
- National and local foundations such as 4-H, Rotary, Kiwanis, YMCA, Boys & Girls Clubs, Women's Auxiliary, American Legion, etc.
- U.S. Veteran's benefits (if your parent is a veteran)
- Occupational interests

There are many resources for financial aid information—all you need to do is use them. As a graduating high school senior planning to continue your education, you may apply for millions of dollars in scholarships. The federal government, along with state higher-education agencies, sponsors three scholarships for high school seniors only. If you qualify, these scholarships can provide you with up to $5,000 per year for college:

Robert C. Byrd Honors Scholarship - Students who demonstrate outstanding academic excellence and leadership skills are eligible to receive this award. Approximately ten or more are given per state annually. Scholarship amounts are usually $1,500 per year for four years of post-secondary education.

Paul Douglas Teacher Scholarship - These scholarships are available to graduating high school seniors in the top ten percent of their class. Recipients who are interested in pursuing a degree in education are eligible to apply. The amount of each award varies, but students can receive up to $5,000 a year. Students are usually required to teach for up to two years in their home state following graduation. If a student decides not to become a teacher after receiving the award, the scholarship simply becomes a loan to be repaid (check to see if your state participates in this program).

National Science Scholars Program (NSSP) - Graduating high school seniors who have achieved academic excellence in the areas of science, mathematics, computer programming, engineering, or related fields are eligible to apply for this scholarship. The NSSP provides funds to students who want to continue study in these areas during college. Each congressional district awards two scholarships for up to $5,000 per year for undergraduate study.

QUICK TIP: *To get more information on these scholarships, contact your state higher education agency (see page 56). Each state will provide you with application information, details, and deadlines about these programs.*

All high school students planning to continue their education must take the PSAT during their junior year. This test not only prepares you for the Scholastic Aptitude Test (SAT) but it may also qualify you for National Merit Scholar status. Becoming a National Merit Scholar can also provide financial assistance for college. One-time awards of $2,000 are given to approximately 2,000 National Merit Scholars.

Financial preparation for college is a four-year process. Students and parents need to begin as early as possible by developing a college financial aid plan. This plan should outline every step that needs to be taken to ensure that the student receives the most aid. Students who stay in touch with their future goals throughout high school have the best chance of receiving aid. Success is achieved by setting deadlines, applying for all aid possible, thoroughly reading the information, and knowing all of the options available. Use the following High School Calendar of Events as a basis for developing a plan that you and your family can follow. This highly useful preparatory calendar contains a wide variety of information for high school students. Of particular importance are these points:

- Do not allow your grades to slip at any time during your high school years. Good grades will enable you to have the best opportunity to win scholarships.

- Make an appointment with a guidance counselor during your sophomore year to discuss future plans.

- Study and be prepared for the PSAT, SAT, and ACT.

- Apply for as many scholarships as you can.

- Before you have been accepted to a particular school, contact all of the schools you are interested in attending and inquire about your financial aid options.

High School Calendar

FRESHMAN YEAR

September–June

- Plan the high school courses you will be taking for all four years with your guidance counselor.
- Set academic goals, and begin your first year of high school with good study habits.

  -Set aside a regular time to study every night

  -Find a quiet place to study without interruption

  -Treat your homework as a part-time job (if you do a little every night, you won't become overwhelmed with assignments!)
- Become involved in extracurricular activities (such as clubs, athletics, student government).
- Begin compiling a list of any awards you receive, activities in which you participate, etc.

SOPHOMORE YEAR

September–May

- Visit your high school counselor or career center to look through college guide catalogs, and select the schools that interest you.
- Contact these schools and ask them to send you brochures and information.
- Compile a list of college costs, including tuition, room and board, books and supplies, for every school in which you are interested.
- Stay involved in outside activities, including after-school jobs.
- Keep your list of activities updated.
- Maintain your grades and good study habits. Your sophomore year grades count towards college admission

June–September

- Study for the PSAT test.

JUNIOR YEAR

September

- Keep studying and register to take the PSAT.
- Talk with your parents and high school counselor to discuss college plans and to make sure you are following the correct steps.
- Send away for more college brochures and financial aid information.

  -Ask for scholarship information from every school you are considering

  -Find out what financial aid forms are required

  -Ask each school if they participate in federally-funded financial aid programs (such as Perkins Loan, Stafford, SEOG)

October

- Take the PSAT to be considered for the National Merit Scholarship.
- Keep up your grades because this is the last full academic year recorded before you apply to colleges.
- Stay involved in extracurricular activities, and keep your list current.

April–May

- Register to take the SAT or ACT tests if the colleges you want to attend require them. This will allow you to retake them if you do not perform well. The next test-taking opportunity is in the fall.

June–September

- Visit as many schools as you can. Make appointments for campus tours, and visit the financial aid office.
- Study for the SAT and ACT. Look into taking a test prep course.

SENIOR YEAR

September

- Send for applications to all of the schools you are interested in attending.
- Start filling out admission applications, making sure you know the application deadlines for out-of-state schools: November; for in-state schools: usually before December.
- Decide which teachers and other people you would like to write a letter of recommendation for you.

  -Be sure to keep a copy of any letters written; you can use them when you apply for scholarships.
- Register for the SAT or ACT.

November

- Financial aid forms are now available from your guidance counselor, financial aid office, or by calling the organizations on page 56.
- Take (or retake) the SAT or ACT.
- Keep your grades up. This semester still counts.

December

- Fill out FAF, AFSA, or both, with your parents' help.

January

- Send your completed financial aid forms to ACT or CSS as soon after January 1 as possible.
- Begin applying for private scholarships and grants.

  -Use your list of activities for reference.

  -Submit copies of your letters of recommendation if requested.

- During this time you should receive notification from the schools to which you applied. Notify the school you have chosen to attend by May 1.
- You'll receive your Student Aid Report (SAR).
  -Make corrections if needed.
  -Send it to the financial aid office at the college of your choice.
- Register for any Advanced Placement tests that you are prepared to take. A good score on several tests can earn you as much as sophomore standing at many colleges.
- After receiving an award letter from the financial aid office at your school, sign it and send it back.
- Apply for any loans you qualify for.

National Phone Directory of Organizations

American Legion Auxiliary
777 North Meridian Street
Indianapolis, IN 46204
(317) 635-6291

Boy Scouts of America
1325 West Walnut Hill Lane
P.O. Box 152079
Irving, TX 75015-2079
(214) 580-2000

Boys and Girls Clubs of America
771 1st Avenue
New York, NY 10017
(212) 351-5900

B.P.O. of the Elks of the United States
(BPOE)
2750 North Lakeview Avenue
Chicago, IL 60614-1889
(312) 477-2750

Fraternal Order of Eagles (FOE)
12660 West Capital Drive
Brookfield, WI 53005
(414) 781-7585

4-H Club of America
National 4-H Center
7100 Connecticut Avenue
Chevy Chase, MD 20815
(301) 961-2840
* Call the local Cooperative Extension
Service Office in your county to find
the nearest 4-H Club.

Girl Scouts of the USA
420 5th Avenue
New York, NY 10018-2702
(212) 852-2000

Kiwanis International
3636 Woodview Trace
Indianapolis, IN 46268
(317) 875-8755

Knights of Columbus
One Columbus Plaza
New Haven, CT 06507
(203) 772-2130

Legionairios del Trabajo in America
Grand Lodge
2154 South San Joaquin Street
Stockton, CA 95206
(209) 463-6516

Lions Club International
300 22nd Street
Oak Brook, IL 60521-8842
(708) 571-5466

National Society of Children of the
American Revolution
1776 D Street NW
Washington, DC 20006-5392
(202) 879-3221

Rotary International
1 Rotary Center
1560 Sherman Avenue
Evanston, IL 60201
(708) 866-3000

Toastmasters International
P.O. Box 9052
Mission Viejo, CA 92690
(714) 858-8255

U.S. Junior Chamber of Commerce
(Jaycees)
P.O. Box 7

Tulsa, OK 74102-0007
(918) 584-2481

Veterans of Foreign Wars (VFW)
406 West 34th Street
Kansas City, MO 64111
(816) 756-3390

Case Study (From High School to an In-State University)

In the middle of his sophomore year of high school, Martin began to think seriously about college. It had always been assumed in his family that he would go, but it wasn't until then that he had thought about where he would go to school or how the costs of his education would be paid. He came from a middle-class family with three children, each one year apart, so he presumed that while his need for financial aid would not be enormous, he would require a small grant or loan to help defray some tuition and living expenses.

SOPHOMORE YEAR

To first determine where he wanted to go to college, he consulted the career counselor at his high school. "That was a first," he said. Figuring that he wanted to live away from home without going too far, he decided to go to an in-state university. He had been an involved student including being on the wrestling team and a member of a community service club. He was planning to run for president of the club. The guidance counselor was the first to tell Martin that these and other activities would help both in the admissions process and in obtaining financial aid. That same year, he began looking into scholarships and grants that might be available to him later, compiling these into a list. He also started maintaining a list of all the activities, clubs, and jobs in which he had been involved since his freshman year.

JUNIOR YEAR

Over the summer, Martin studied for the PSAT, which he would take in October. "I was a little worried about it, because I've never done great on those standardized tests, but the preparation really helped.", he said. He decided to take the SAT and ACT the following spring for practice. Junior year brought another meeting with his counselor to discuss applying to schools and for financial aid. Martin made sure to keep his grades as high as possible, and, in late fall, he became vice-president of Interact.

After taking the tests in the spring, he felt he needed to take an SAT prep course, so he signed up for one that summer, completing it in just a few weeks. He kept his activities list updated, and decided on seven schools to which he wanted to apply. He then called each one, requesting information on tuition, expenses, and financial aid, and asking whether they accepted the FAF or the AFSA. He brought this information to his parents so they could determine how much they could contribute and how much aid he would need, based on the costs of each school.

When his senior year began, Martin sent applications to all seven colleges and retook both the SAT and ACT. The tests, he said, " were much easier the second time around." He submitted a request shortly after November 1 for the FAF and AFSA, filling them out with the help of his parents. The applications were mailed on January 2, the earliest they could be submitted. He also applied for several scholarships, citing all his many activities. Within a few months, he had received his Student Aid Report (SAR), indicating he was eligible to receive a Pell Grant. Spring also brought acceptances from five of the universities that had interested him. Choosing the right school "was definitely the hardest part of the whole process.", he said. Once that decision was made, he sent his SAR to the financial aid office at the college of his choice.

Martin's expenses were projected to total $5,690, including all tuition, books, and accommodations. He received a $1,200 Pell Grant and $2,000 from the Perkins Loan program. His aid was this high because he had two siblings who would be attending college at the same time, putting quite a financial burden on his family. He additionally received $1,500 in scholarships in response to the many applications he submitted.

Martin currently attends a large university with a top-ranked wrestling program. He will reapply next year for continuing aid.

Case Study (Applying to a Private School)

Joanne, having graduated from high school, wasn't sure what major she wanted to pursue or even what kind of school she wanted to attend. Not wanting to waste time and money taking courses that might not be useful to her later, she elected to postpone college until she decided on her goals. She worked as a waitress for two years, living on her own and establishing her independence. When it came time to apply for financial aid, this meant that only her income and not her family's would be used to calculate her monetary need. This was an important factor because her father, who had not attended college himself, did not want to help pay for her higher education, thinking it unnecessary.

The two years on her own allowed Joanne to save about $1,500 and sort out her career path. She opted to apply to a small, private arts college in a major urban area to seek a theater degree. Yearly tuition at the school was approximately $8,000, so she knew that she would not be able to attend without substantial assistance. Immediately upon being accepted, she filled out the FAF and had a copy sent to her prospective school. She didn't apply to any private sources for scholarships; in her words, "I didn't think there was anyone who wanted to give money to an aspiring actor." The school examined her financial report and sent her an award letter which indicated her total need as $12,600, including tuition, books, room and board, transportation, and personal expenses. They offered her aid as follows:

Pell Grant	$2,400
Stafford Loan	$2,625
Supplemental Educational Opportunity Grant	$599
Perkins Loan	$681
Work-Study Program	$2,895
Trustee Grant	$400
Total	**$9,600**

The disparity between her perceived need and the amount they offered was made up partially through her savings and partially, she said, "by living very frugally. I ate a lot of macaroni and cheese." Joanne spent about fifteen hours each week working on campus to fulfill her work-study requirements, cleaning classrooms and working in the school deli. Time demands of classes and rehearsals didn't allow her to work additionally during the school year.

She had a few different jobs during the summers, which she sometimes found by checking the bulletin boards in her financial aid office. These included being a receptionist at an employment agency and working in the frame shop of an art gallery. She even was able to occasionally act in industrial and educational films, which paid up to $250 for just a day or two of work. "I was fortunate to live in a city with decent employment opportunities, especially for actors," she said. By saving money in the summers and continuing to live moderately, she was able to offset the difference between her perceived need and aid offered each year. Small tuition increases were counteracted by equivalent increases in her loan and grant awards.

By Joanne's senior year, she was aware of the many scholarship options, so she applied for several and was awarded $2,500. Because her award was based on merit, not need, the rest of her financial aid remained the same. Her good grades and acting talent had paid off. She said, "I felt like blowing the money on a stereo or a trip to Europe. I was sick of old clothes and public transportation." Wisely, she instead accepted less loan money that year to decrease her post-graduation debt.

Joanne is now performing for a repertory theater company as a paid intern. She ultimately plans to go to graduate school for a masters degree in fine arts, and hopes for the passage of President Clinton's financial aid reform program. "Filling out all those forms year after year was a real pain. The system is pretty much a hassle, but I wouldn't have a college degree without it."

Case Study (Applying to an Out-of-State School)

During her senior year of high school, Allison decided to attend college in another state because the universities in her state did not offer satisfactory programs in communications. She realized that this decision meant increased tuition costs—possibly tripling the cost of a local school—and so she sought financial assistance. First, she contacted the financial aid office at the university and asked which financial aid forms they required. Next, she requested a list of estimated student expenses for the year. Using this information, she determined her yearly expenses as approximately $15,000 including tuition, room and board, books, supplies, transportation, and personal expenses. She received the required FAF form, completed it, and submitted it in early January.

Allison received her Student Aid Report (SAR) four weeks after sending in the FAF. The SAR contained information on her eligibility for a Pell Grant, so she sent the SAR to the university for further processing. Allison made an essential contact while calling the financial aid office at the university to confirm the receipt of her forms. She said, "By knowing someone by name and being friendly with her, I got less of a run-around. It was much easier to receive information that way." She also needed loans, so she requested information about lending institutions from the financial aid office. She completed and sent the forms to both the school and the lenders. When she received her award letter, it listed the following aid:

Pell Grant	$2,400
Stafford Loan	$2,250
Perkins Loan	$3,000
College Work Study	$3,000
Student Contribution	$1,200
Parental Contribution	$2,000
TOTAL	**$13,850**

Because she has a twin sister in college, her aid was higher than it would have been if she were an only child. The amount of parental contribution is considerably lower when more than one child attends college. Allison's savings covered the excess need and she found a job by checking the bulletin board in the financial aid office at school. She worked for a campus museum for twenty hours a week to fulfill her work-study obligation, and says it didn't interfere with her studies. In January of her freshman year, she filed for financial aid again and received virtually the same type and amount of aid.

Her parents did not claim Allison as a dependent on their income tax forms that year, thus enabling her to establish residency. Requirements for residency differ in each state and in her case she needed to live and work in-state for twelve consecutive months. She achieved resident status by her junior year and her tuition decreased from $2,700 to $720 per quarter. Unfortunately, she turned her aid application in late and lost eligibility for a Perkins Loan. However, the amount of free aid she received did not decrease; she simply required less loan money. Allison also left her work-study job that year. "It was great, but I wanted to do something more related to communications." She found part-time internships at a television station and a publishing company.

Aid for her senior year was essentially unchanged. She continued her internships and studies, and graduated on time with a degree in communications. Allison is currently looking for a career in either print or broadcast media. "Or maybe I'll just go to Tibet until the job market improves."

Forms

Student Financial Services

Filling Out Forms

Unfortunately, students are unable to receive financial aid through a phone call alone. As previously indicated in the federal aid section, application forms are required for any kind of collegiate financial assistance program. These forms can be daunting, and as a result, many students avoid filing for financial aid. Don't be intimidated, because once you actually begin, there are very few difficulties, particularly if you carefully follow the directions. If you have read and understood the information contained in the federal aid section, you will know how to approach this section. The material is organized to give you specific tips for completing the FAF and AFSA application forms.

You will learn:

- What each form looks like.

- The correct form to complete for each type of government grant or loan.

- Who to call if you run into difficulty. There are people you can turn to for answers to questions about particular parts of the application.

- How and where to obtain these forms and where to send them upon completion.

- Which sections of each form are most important (or most confusing), and how to deal with specific problems.

Complete and return the forms well in advance of the required deadlines so you can be assured of receiving some type of financial aid.

QUICK TIP: *Financial Aid forms can be obtained after November 1 of every year from your financial aid counselor, the college or university you are planning to attend, or from your state agency (see page 56 for information). Remember, do not submit your application until after January 1 or it will be returned to you unprocessed.*

New financial aid laws require your parents to provide financial information on the application, whether or not you are classified as independent from them. If you answer "no" to every question, your parents must complete the parent information sections.

- Were you born before January 1, 1970?   Yes_____ No_____
- Are you a graduate or professional student?   Yes_____ No_____
- Are you a veteran of the armed forces?   Yes_____ No_____
- Are you married?   Yes_____ No_____
- Are both your parents deceased or are you a ward of the Court?   Yes_____ No_____
- Do you have legal dependents other than a spouse?   Yes_____ No_____

If you answered "yes" to any of these questions, you are only required to fill out the student sections of the financial aid forms. Be prepared to provide parental documentation if requested!

FORM COMPLETION: GENERAL RULES

Prior to Completing the Forms

- The **FIRST** step is to call the financial aid office at your college or university to determine which form is required (AFSA, FAF, another form, or a combination of forms). When you contact the school, ask these two very important questions:

  1. What is the financial aid deadline for college aid?

2. What is the financial aid deadline for state aid?

- If you have not yet decided which school to attend, and if each school requires a different financial aid application, choose one form to complete and call CSS at (609) 951-1025 to have a duplicate copy of your SAR sent to the other institutions.

- Ask for two copies of any requested form. Students often make mistakes during their first attempt to complete the form or, worse yet, they misplace the form.

- Photocopy all parts of each form and use these copies as rough drafts. Be sure, however, to send only the original form back to the appropriate address (as listed on the form).

Gather all financial data that may be needed:

- 1993 U.S. Income Tax Return

    -If your return isn't completed before you apply for aid, estimate your income and expected earnings

    -You'll need your return, your parents' return, and your spouse's return

- W-2 Forms and other records of earned income during the previous year

- Records of untaxed income

- Bank statements

- Records of benefits received through Department of Veterans' Affairs, Social Security, and any other federal or state agency

- Records of investments (such as stocks, bonds, property, savings)

- Mortgage information

- Medical and dental expenses for the previous year

- Farm or business records

- Driver's license and social security numbers

- Information on financial aid already received (student loan balances)

QUICK TIP: *It is very important that you retain all of these documents in case you are asked to provide proof of information contained in your aid application. If you can't document your claims, you won't receive any federal or state assistance. In other words, save everything.*

Completing the Forms

- Use a No. 2 pencil on the FAF and a black ballpoint pen on the AFSA. Do not use felt tip pens, markers, or colored pencils. For other forms, read instructions carefully.

- If you make a mistake, be sure to erase it with a clean eraser only. Do not use "white out" or any other correction fluid.

- Complete all sections and leave no question blank unless otherwise requested. Place an 'N/A' or '0' in spaces without responses.

- Always use exact figures. If this is not possible, use estimated figures. Do not enter a range of figures (such as $500 to $1,000).

- Never put two separate amounts in one answer blank.

- Do not write in the margins of the forms, because this could cause the computer to register incorrect information.

- Be sure that everyone who provided information to you for the completion of the form places his or her signature in the appropriate section.

Mailing the Forms

- Do not return completed forms that have been torn, crumpled, or stained because the computer will be unable to scan them properly.

- Send the original application, but make a copy of the completed form for your own records.

- Do not send any extra materials such as tax forms or letters along with the required forms. Send only the form and the processing fee. If you would like to make comments, do so only in the appropriate section.

- Do not send any form via certified or registered mail. Students (or parents) who do this slow up the process.

- Never staple your check or money order directly to the application.

QUICK TIP: *If ever in doubt, refer to this checklist, talk to your financial aid advisor, or call (800) 4FED-AID. Your every effort should be focused on completing each aid application correctly the first time. Those who do not can expect both delays and extra work.*

At the time of this printing, no planned changes to either the FAF or AFSA have been announced in response to the new 1993-1994 federal financial aid bill.

The Financial Aid Form (FAF)

The FAF is one of the most commonly used application forms for those applying to non-federal and federal aid programs. Completed applications are processed by a privately-run company called the College Scholarship Service (CSS). The FAF asks you to report information including income and assets (for both you and your parents if you are a dependent), which is then used to evaluate your "financial need." After processing your form, CSS will send it to the colleges of your choice and to the U.S. Department of Education. If you are applying only for Federal Aid, there is no charge for the processing of the form, but if you request that the results be sent to any colleges, a service fee will be charged. The cost of this service charge depends on the number of colleges you want to receive your FAF information. The fees range from $9.75 for one college to $64 for eight. Deadlines must be met without exception. If you are applying for federal or state aid, you must complete and return the form as soon after January 1 as possible, and no later than May 2, 1994.

QUICK TIP: *This year, ACT discontinued the use of the Family Financial Statement form (FFS). Schools nationwide now use either the FAF, AFSA, or both, depending on the type of aid offered. Before you begin, contact the financial aid office at the college or university you are planning to attend to find out which form they require.*

THE FAF IS USED FOR THESE PROGRAMS:

- State Aid
- Federal Aid
  -Pell Grants
  -SEOG Grants
  -College Work Study

-Perkins Loans

-Stafford Loans

TIPS FOR COMPLETING THE FAF

- Read and understand all the information presented before you begin to filling out your FAF.

- Take it a section at a time. Don't read ahead. The best way to fill out the FAF accurately is to follow the instructions that correspond to the section you are completing. Use the copies provided.

- Use a No. 2 pencil when completing the FAF.

- Be sure to fill out all the white sections.

- Questions in blue are asking for parental information; questions in white are asking about student information.

   - If you are unclear about your parents' need to provide information, refer to page 150 of this book.

- If you are a high school senior applying for financial aid, you must fill in question six with a code number for your high school. See your high school financial aid or guidance counselor for that six-digit number.

- If you are filing both an FAF and AFSA, FAF filers must complete questions 45c and 45d on the AFSA form, even if instructions say to skip them.

- All who have provided information for use on the form must sign it in the certification area on page 4. Do not forget this important step!

- Section L on the FAF allows you to request that your financial information be sent to eight colleges. Later, your FAF information can be sent to more schools by using the Additional College Request form (ACR). You'll receive this form with your SAR approximately four weeks from the date your application was submitted.

- The correct service fee must be included with the application if you would like CSS to send information to any colleges that you have listed.

- Use Section M on the FAF to explain any unusual financial circumstances (such as medical bills not covered by insurance, serious illness, or loss of employment) that affect your (or your parents') ability to cover your college expenses.

- If you, your parents, or spouse qualify as a dislocated worker, use section M to explain.

- Before you return the completed FAF application, go through the checklist below to make sure you have correctly filled out the form.

   ❏ Have you printed your name correctly on the top of page 2?

   ❏ Has everyone who provided information on the form signed their name on the bottom of page 4?

   ❏ Did you fill in your social security number in question 5?

   ❏ Are you enclosing the correct processing fee?

   ❏ Did you make a copy of the FAF for your own records?

❑ Are you sending the undamaged original?

❑ Did you put two 29 cent stamps on the envelope?

❑ Are you sending your application in as soon as possible after January 1?

For more information concerning the FAF application process or the status of your application, or to request an additional copy of the FAF, contact your financial aid counselor or call CSS at (301) 722-9200.

Use the following FAF form as a practice application. Once completed, transfer the information to an original FAF using a No. 2 pencil, and send it to:

Federal Student Aid Programs
P.O. Box 6376
Princeton, NJ 08541

FAF

FAF® Financial Aid Form — 1993-94   ☐ ☐

> This form is not required to apply for Title IV federal student aid. However, information from the FAF is used by some colleges and private organizations to award their own financial aid funds. CSS charges students a fee to collect and report this information. By filling out this form, you are agreeing to pay the fee, which is calculated in question 44.

Section A — Student's Identification Information — Be sure to complete this section. Answer the questions the same way you answered them in Section A of the Free Application for Federal Student Aid (FAFSA).

1. Your name
Last   First   M.I.

3. Title (optional)
1 ☐ Mr.   2 ☐ Miss, Ms., or Mrs.

2. Your permanent mailing address (Mail will be sent to this address.)
Number, street, and apartment number

City   State   Zip Code

4. Your date of birth
Month   Day   Year

5. Your social security number
☐☐☐ – ☐☐ – ☐☐☐☐

Section B — Student's Other Information

6. If you are now in high school, give your high school 6-digit code number.

7. What year will you be in college in 1993-94? (Mark only one box.)

1 ☐ 1st (never previously attended college)
2 ☐ 1st (previously attended college)
3 ☐ 2nd
4 ☐ 3rd
5 ☐ 4th

6 ☐ 5th or more undergraduate
7 ☐ first-year graduate/professional (beyond a bachelor's degree)
8 ☐ second-year graduate/professional
9 ☐ third-year graduate/professional
0 ☐ fourth-year or more graduate/ professional

8. a. If you have previously attended any college or other postsecondary school, write in the total number of colleges and schools you have attended. ☐

b. List below the colleges (up to five) that you have attended. Begin with the college you attended most recently. Use the CSS code numbers from the list in the FAF instruction booklet. If more space is needed, use Section M.

Name, city, and state of college	Period of attendance From (mo./yr.)	To (mo./yr.)	CSS Code Number
			☐☐☐
			☐☐☐
			☐☐☐
			☐☐☐
			☐☐☐

9. During the 1993-94 school year, you want institutional financial aid
from ☐☐ ☐☐ through ☐☐ ☐☐
Month Year   Month Year

10. Mark your preference for institutional work and/or loan assistance.

1 ☐ Part-time job only
2 ☐ Loan only
3 ☐ Will accept both, but prefer loan
4 ☐ Will accept both, but prefer job
5 ☐ No preference

11. If it is necessary to borrow money to pay for educational expenses, do you want to be considered for a Stafford Loan? (optional)   Yes ☐ 1   No ☐ 2

(If you mark "Yes," your information may be sent to the loan agency within your state.)

12. a. Your employer/occupation _____

b. Employer's address _____

c. Will you continue to work for this employer during the 1993-94 school year? Yes ☐ 1   No ☐ 2

13. If you have dependents other than a spouse, how many will be in each of the following age groups during 1993-94?

Ages 0-5 ☐   Ages 6-12 ☐   Ages 13+ ☐

14. 1992 child support paid by you $_____ .00

Section C — Student's Expected Summer/School-Year Income

	Summer 1993 3 months	School Year 1993-94 9 months		Summer 1993 3 months	School Year 1993-94 9 months
15. Income earned from work by you	$_____ .00	$_____ .00	**17.** Other taxable income	$_____ .00	$_____ .00
16. Income earned from work by spouse	$_____ .00	$_____ .00	**18.** Nontaxable income and benefits	$_____ .00	$_____ .00

FAF (continued)

Section D — Student's (& Spouse's) Assets

	What is it worth today?	What is owed on it?

19. Cash and checking accounts $ _____ .00

21. Other real estate $ _____ .00 $ _____ .00

20. Home (Renters write in "0.")   What is it worth today? $ _____ .00   What is owed on it? $ _____ .00

22. Investments & savings (See instructions.) $ _____ .00 $ _____ .00

Section E — Family Members' Listing
Give information for all family members but don't give information about yourself. List up to seven other family members here. If there are more than seven, list first those who will be in college at least half-time. List the others in Section M.

23.

#	Full name of family member You — the Student Applicant	Age	Relationship (Use code below*)	In the 1993-94 school year, will attend college for at least one term full-time / half-time	Name of school or college this person will attend in 1993-94 school year	Year in school 1993-94	If attended college in 1992-93, give amount of: 1992-93 Scholarships/Grants	1992-93 Parents' Contribution
1				1 ☐ 2 ☐				
2				1 ☐ 2 ☐				
3				1 ☐ 2 ☐				
4				1 ☐ 2 ☐				
5				1 ☐ 2 ☐				
6				1 ☐ 2 ☐				
7				1 ☐ 2 ☐				
8				1 ☐ 2 ☐				

Write in the correct code from below. ↑

* Relationship Codes:
1 = Student's parent   3 = Student's brother/stepbrother or sister/stepsister   5 = Student's son or daughter   7 = Other (Explain in Section M.)
2 = Student's stepparent   4 = Student's husband or wife   6 = Student's grandparent

If you were directed to provide parents' information when you completed the Free Application for Federal Student Aid, you should also give parents' information in the following sections. Some colleges may require your parents' information even if you were not directed to provide it on the Free Application for Federal Student Aid. See page 5 of the FAF instruction booklet if you are unsure about whether you should provide parents' information.

Section F — Parents' Information — See page 5 of the FAF instruction booklet.

24. Check one: ☐ Father ☐ Stepfather ☐ Legal Guardian ☐ Other - Explain in Section M.

25. Check one: ☐ Mother ☐ Stepmother ☐ Legal Guardian ☐ Other - Explain in Section M.

a. Name _____ Age [‖]

a. Name _____ Age [‖]

b. Occupation/Employer _____ No. years _____

b. Occupation/Employer _____ No. years _____

26. Parent(s) address (if different from address in question 2):   Street address: _____

City/State/Zip: _____

Section G — Divorced, Separated, or Remarried Parents
(To be answered by the parent who completes this form, if the student's natural or adoptive parents are divorced, separated, or remarried.)

27. a. Year of separation [‖]   Year of divorce [‖]

b. Other parent's name _____

Home address _____

_____

_____

Occupation/Employer _____

_____

_____

c. According to court order, when will support for the student end? [‖] [‖] Month Year

d. Who last claimed the student as a tax exemption? _____

In which year? [‖]

e. Is there an agreement specifying a contribution for the student's education?   Yes ☐   No ☐

If yes, how much for the 1993-94 school year? $ _____ .00

FAF (continued)

Section H — Parents' 1992 Taxable Income & Expenses

28. Breakdown of 1992 Adjusted Gross Income (AGI)

Tax Filers Only

a. Wages, salaries, tips (IRS Form 1040 — line 7, 1040A — line 7, or 1040EZ — line 1) 28a. $ _____ .00

b. Interest income (IRS Form 1040 — line 8a, 1040A — line 8a, or 1040EZ — line 2) b. $ _____ .00

c. Dividend income (IRS Form 1040 — line 9 or 1040A — line 9) c. $ _____ .00

d. Net income (or loss) from business, farm, rents, royalties, partnerships, estates, trusts, etc. (IRS Form 1040 — lines 12, 18, and 19). If a loss, enter the amount in (parentheses). d. $ _____ .00

e. Other taxable income such as alimony received, capital gains (or losses), pensions, annuities, etc. (IRS Form 1040 — lines 10, 11, 13-15, 16b, 17b, 20, 21b, and 22 or 1040A — lines 10b, 11b, 12, and 13b) e. $ _____ .00

f. Adjustments to income (IRS Form 1040 — line 30 or 1040A — line 15c) f. $ _____ .00

29. 1992 child support paid by parent(s) completing this form. 29. $ _____ .00

30. 1992 medical and dental expenses not covered by insurance. 30. $ _____ .00

31. 1992 total elementary, junior high school, and high school tuition paid for dependent children. 31. $ _____ .00

Section I — Parents' 1992 Untaxed Income & Benefits

32. Write in below your other untaxed 1992 income and benefits.

a. Deductible IRA and/or Keogh payments from Form 1040, total of lines 24a, 24b, and 27 or 1040A, line 15c $ _____ .00

b. Payments to tax-deferred pension and savings plans (paid directly or withheld from earnings) Include untaxed portions of 401(k) and 403(b) plans. $ _____ .00

c. Earned income credit from Form 1040, line 56 or 1040A, line 28c $ _____ .00

d. Housing, food, and other living allowances (excluding rent subsidies for low-income housing) paid to members of the military, clergy, and others (Include cash payments and cash value of benefits.) $ _____ .00

e. Tax-exempt interest income from Form 1040, line 8b or 1040A, line 8b $ _____ .00

f. Untaxed portions of pensions from Form 1040, line 16a minus 16b and line 17a minus 17b or 1040A, line 10a minus 10b and line 11a minus 11b (excluding "rollovers") $ _____ .00

g. Foreign income exclusion from Form 2555, line 39 $ _____ .00

h. Credit for federal tax on special fuels from Form 4136–Part III: Total Income Tax Credit $ _____ .00

i. Any other untaxed income and benefits (See instructions.) $ _____ .00

Section J — Parents' 1993 Expected Income

33. 1993 income earned from work by father $ _____ .00

34. 1993 income earned from work by mother $ _____ .00

35. 1993 other taxable income $ _____ .00

36. 1993 nontaxable income and benefits $ _____ .00

Section K — Parents' Assets

37. Cash and checking accounts $ _____ .00

38. If parents own home, give

    a. year purchased | 1 | 9 | | | b. purchase price $ _____ .00

39. Parents' monthly home mortgage or rental payment (If none, explain in Section M.) $ _____ .00

	What is it worth today?	What is owed on it?
40. Home (Renters write in "0.")	$ _____ .00	$ _____ .00
41. Other real estate	$ _____ .00	$ _____ .00
42. Investments & savings (See instructions.)	$ _____ .00	$ _____ .00

FAF (continued)

Section L — Student's Colleges & Programs

43. List the names and CSS code numbers of up to eight colleges and programs to which you want CSS to send information from this form and from the Free Application for Federal Student Aid. Enclose the right fee. See the FAF instructions and **44**.

Name	City and State	CSS Code No.	Housing Code*

*Housing Codes for 1993-94 (Enter only one code for each college.)
1 = With parents   2 = Campus housing   3 = Off-campus housing   4 = With relatives

44. Fee: Mark the box that tells how many colleges and programs are listed in **43**.

CSS Only

1 ☐ $9.75   3 ☐ $25.25   5 ☐ $40.75   7 ☐ $56.25
2 ☐ $17.50   4 ☐ $33.00   6 ☐ $48.50   8 ☐ $64.00

Make out your check or money order for the total amount above to the College Scholarship Service. Return this form, the fee, and the Free Application for Federal Student Aid in the mailing envelope that came with your FAFSA/FAF. **You must send the correct fee with your FAF. If you fail to do so, the FAF will be returned to you unprocessed. However, CSS will process your FAFSA without a fee.**

Section M — Explanations/Special Circumstances
Use this space to explain any unusual expenses such as high medical or dental expenses, educational and other debts, or special circumstances.

Don't send letters, tax forms, or other materials with your FAF as they will be destroyed.

Certification:
All the information on this form is true and complete to the best of my knowledge. If asked by an authorized official, I agree to give proof of the information that I have given on this form. I realize that this proof may include a copy of my U.S., state, or local income tax returns. I also realize that if I don't give proof when asked, the student may not get aid. I give permission to send information from my FAFSA and FAF to the colleges and programs in **43**.

Everyone giving information on this form must sign below.

1 _____   2 _____
Student's signature   Student's spouse's signature

3 _____   4 _____
Father's (Stepfather's) signature   Mother's (Stepmother's) signature

When you have completed this form, make a copy for your records.

Date this form was completed:
Month Day   1 ☐ 1993   2 ☐ 1994   Year
Write in the month and day. Mark the year completed.

Page 4

21701-02592 • CW122M

The Application for Federal Student Aid (AFSA)

The AFSA is used only by those applying for federal aid. Some colleges or universities will allow you to use this form to apply for state aid. Contact the financial aid office at your school to see if they accept the AFSA to determine college and state aid eligibility. This form is processed by the U.S. Department of Education (not by a private company), and is used to determine an applicant's "financial need" and Pell Grant Index. The form is free and can be obtained from your school's financial aid office, or by calling (800) 4FED-AID. There is no service charge for the processing of the form, but the information is not sent to the schools of your choice. If the school needs this information, they will request it from the Department of Education. Any specific questions or requests concerning the AFSA are handled by the Federal Student Aid Financial Center at (800) 4-FED-AID. This government service is very helpful, and a representative may offer to guide you step-by-step through the form. The AFSA needs to be sent in as soon after January 1 as possible, and no later than May 2, 1994. If you desire financial aid, do not miss the deadline (there are no exceptions).

THE AFSA IS USED FOR THESE PROGRAMS:

Federal Aid:

- Pell Grants
- SEOG Grants
- College Work Study
- Perkins Loans
- Stafford Loans

QUICK TIP: *The AFSA application can now be filed electronically at over 3,000 colleges and universities nationwide. This has made the application process quicker, easier, and almost without errors. Check with the financial aid office at your school to see if they participate in this program.*

Tips for Completing the AFSA

- Read and understand all the information presented before you begin filling out your AFSA.

- Use a pen with black or dark ink; do not use a pencil. Be sure that you complete a practice copy (on a photocopy of the form) because you cannot correct mistakes on the original form.

- Don't read all of the instructions before completing the form. The best way to fill out the AFSA accurately is to follow only the instructions that correspond to the section you're completing.

- Questions that are outlined in green are asking for parental information; questions in grey are asking about student information.

  -If you are unsure about whether your parents need to provide financial information, refer to page 15 of this book.

- Make sure that you include your social security number, or your application may not be processed.

- Be sure each person who contributed information signs the form in the blank for question 35.

- There is no charge for the processing of this form, so do not send money (it will not be returned).

- If you fall into the following categories, there are some questions on the AFSA that you may not have to answer.

  -If every member of your family files a 1993 1040A or 1040EZ, or doesn't file any 1993 U.S. income tax at all and...

  -If your family's gross income is less than $50,000 a year.

- If your school accepts the AFSA to determine state and college aid eligibility, you must complete all of sections G & I.

- Do not complete the "Preparer's Use" section. This is to be completed by the person who reviews the form.

- Before you send in your completed AFSA application, go through this checklist to make sure you have correctly filled out the form.

  ❑ Has everyone who provided information on the form signed question 35, section G?

  ❑ If you are also submitting an FAF, have you answered questions 45c and 45d?

  ❑ Did you fill in your social security number on question 5, section A?

  ❑ Did you make a copy of the AFSA for your own records?

  ❑ Are you sending in the original form?

  ❑ Did you put two 29 cent stamps on the envelope?

  ❑ Are you sending your application as soon as possible after January 1?

The following AFSA form is a practice application. Complete it, then transfer the information onto an original AFSA with a black pen, and send it to:

Federal Student Aid Programs
P.O. Box 6376
Princeton, NJ 08541

If you have any questions about the completion or deadlines of the AFSA, contact a financial aid counselor at your college or university or call (800) 4FED-AID.

AFSA

Free Application for Federal Student Aid

1994-95 School Year

WARNING: If you purposely give false or misleading information on this form, you may be fined $10,000, sent to prison, or both.

"You" and "your" on this form always mean the student who wants aid.

A A A A A

Form Approved
OMB No. 1840-0110
APP. EXP. 6/30/95

U.S. Department of Education
Student Financial
Assistance Programs

Section A: Yourself

1-3. Your name

1. Last   **2.** First   **3.** M.I.

Your title (optional)   Mr. ☐₁   Miss, Ms., or Mrs. ☐₂

4-7. Your permanent mailing address (*All mail will be sent to this address. See Instructions, page 2 for state/country abbreviations.*)

4. Number and street (Include apt. no.)

5. City   **6.** State   **7.** ZIP code

8. Your permanent home telephone number   Area code

9. Your state of legal residence   State

10. Date you became a legal resident of the state in question 9 (*See Instructions, page 2.*)   Month   Day   Year

11-12. Your driver's license number (*Include the state abbreviation. If you don't have a license, leave this question blank.*)   State

13. Your social security number (*Don't leave blank. See Instructions, page 3.*)

14. Your date of birth   Month   Day   Year

15-16. Are you a U.S. citizen? (*See Instructions, page 3.*)

Yes, I am a U.S. citizen. ☐₁

No, but I am an eligible noncitizen. ☐₂

A

No, neither of the above. ☐₃

17. As of **today**, are you married? (*Check only one box.*)

I am not married. (I am single, widowed, or divorced.) ☐₁

I am married. ☐₂

I am separated from my spouse. ☐₃

18. Date you were married, widowed, separated, or divorced. If divorced, use earliest date of divorce or separation.   Month   Year

19. Will you have your first bachelor's degree before July 1, 1994?   Yes ☐₁ No ☐₂

Section B: Your Plans

20. Your year in college during the 1994-95 school year (*Check only one box.*)

1st ☐₁   3rd ☐₃   5th year or more undergraduate ☐₅

2nd ☐₂   4th ☐₄   graduate ☐₆

21-24. Your expected enrollment status for the 1994-95 school year (*See Instructions, page 3.*)

School term	Full time	3/4 time	1/2 time	Less than 1/2 time	Not enrolled
21. Summer term '94	☐₁	☐₂	☐₃	☐₄	☐₅
22. Fall sem./quarter '94	☐₁	☐₂	☐₃	☐₄	☐₅
23. Winter quarter '94-'95	☐₁	☐₂	☐₃	☐₄	☐₅
24. Spring sem./quarter '95	☐₁	☐₂	☐₃	☐₄	☐₅

25-26. Your degree/certificate and course of study (*See Instructions, page 3.*)

25. Degree/certificate

26. Course of study

27. Date you expect to complete your degree/certificate   Month   Day   Year

28-30. In addition to grants, what other types of financial aid are you (and your parents) interested in? (*Check one or more boxes.*)

• Work-study ☐₁

• Student loans ☐₂

• Parent loans for students (Federal PLUS) ☐₃

31. If you are (or were) in college, do you plan to attend **that same college** in 1994-95?

Yes ☐₁ No ☐₂

32. For how many dependent children will you pay child care expenses in 1994-95?

33-34. Veterans education benefits you expect to receive from July 1, 1994 through June 30, 1995

33. Amount per month $_____.00

34. Number of months

AFSA (continued)

Section C: Education Background

35–36. Date that you (the student) received, or will receive, your high school diploma, either—

- by graduating from high school
OR
     ☐☐ ☐☐
     Month   Year

- by earning a GED
     ☐☐ ☐☐
     Month   Year

(Enter one date. Leave blank if the question does not apply to you.)

37–38. Highest grade level completed by your father and your mother *(Check one box for each parent. See Instructions, page 4.)*

	37. Father	**38.** Mother
elementary school (K–8)	☐₁	☐₁
high school (9–12)	☐₂	☐₂
college or beyond	☐₃	☐₃
unknown	☐₄	☐₄

Section D: Federal Family Education Loan (FFEL) Program Information

(Leave this section blank if you have never received a Federal Stafford Loan, a Guaranteed Student Loan [GSL], or a Federal Insured Student Loan [FISL].)

39. If you borrowed under the Federal Stafford, Federal SLS, Federal PLUS, or Federal Consolidation Loan program and there is an outstanding balance on your loan(s), enter the date of your oldest outstanding loan.

     ☐☐ ☐☐
     Month   Year

42. Check one box to indicate the interest rate you have on your outstanding Federal Stafford Loan.

7% ☐₁   9% ☐₃   Variable ☐₅

8% ☐₂   8%/10% ☐₄

40–41. Write in the total outstanding balance(s) on your Federal Stafford and Federal SLS Loans.

Amount owed

    40.   Federal Stafford Loan(s) $_____.00

    41.   Federal SLS Loan(s) $_____.00

43–44. Do you currently have a Federal PLUS Loan or a Consolidation Loan?

	Yes	No
43. Federal PLUS Loan	☐₁	☐₂
44. Federal Consolidation Loan	☐₁	☐₂

Section E: Student Status

	Yes	No
45. Were you born **before** January 1, 1971?	☐₁	☐₂
46. Are you a veteran of the U.S. Armed Forces?	☐₁	☐₂
47. Will you be a graduate or professional student in 1994-95?	☐₁	☐₂
48. Are you married?	☐₁	☐₂
49. Are you a ward of the court or are both your parents dead?	☐₁	☐₂
50. Do you have legal dependents (*other than a spouse*) that fit the definition in Instructions, page 4?	☐₁	☐₂

If you answered **"Yes"** to **any** question in Section E, go to Section F and fill out the **GRAY** and the **WHITE** areas on the rest of the form.

If you answered **"No"** to **every** question in Section E, go to Section F, and fill out the **BLUE** and the **WHITE** areas on the rest of the form.

Section F: Household Information

If you are filling out the GRAY and WHITE areas, answer questions 51 and 52, and go to Section G.

If you are filling out the BLUE and WHITE areas, skip questions 51 and 52. Answer questions 53 through 57 about your parents, and then go on to Section G.

STUDENT (& SPOUSE)

51. Number of family members in 1994-95 (Include yourself and your spouse. Include your children and other people only if they meet the definition in Instructions, page 5.)
  ☐☐

52. Number of college students in 1994-95 (Of the number in 51, how many will be in college at least half-time for at least one term? Include yourself. *See Instructions, page 5.*)
  ☐☐

PARENTS

53. Your parents' current marital status:

single ☐₁   separated ☐₃   widowed ☐₅

married ☐₂   divorced ☐₄

54. Your parents' state of legal residence ☐☐

55. Date your parent(s) became legal resident(s) of the state in question 54
(See Instructions, page 5.)
  ☐☐ ☐☐ ☐☐
  Month   Day   Year

56. Number of family members in 1994-95 (Include yourself and your parents. Include your parents' other children and other people only if they meet the definition in Instructions, page 5.)
  ☐☐

57. Number of college students in 1994-95 (Of the number in 56, how many will be in college at least half-time for at least one term? Include yourself. *See Instructions, page 6.*)
  ☐☐

AFSA (continued)

Section G: 1993 Income, Earnings, and Benefits   Everyone must fill out the Student (& Spouse) column.   *Page 3*
*(You **must** see the instructions for income and taxes that you should exclude from questions in this section.)*

STUDENT (& SPOUSE)	PARENTS
58. The following 1993 U.S. income tax figures are from: *(Check only one box.)*	**69.** The following 1993 U.S. income tax figures are from: *(Check only one box.)*

STUDENT (& SPOUSE)		PARENTS	
a completed 1993 IRS Form 1040A or 1040EZ	(Go to 59) ☐₁	a completed 1993 IRS Form 1040A or 1040EZ (Go to 70) ☐₁
a completed 1993 IRS Form 1040	(Go to 59) ☐₂	a completed 1993 IRS Form 1040 (Go to 70) ☐₂
an estimated 1993 IRS Form 1040A or 1040EZ	(Go to 59) ☐₃	an estimated 1993 IRS Form 1040A or 1040EZ (Go to 70) ☐₃
an estimated 1993 IRS Form 1040	(Go to 59) ☐₄	an estimated 1993 IRS Form 1040 (Go to 70) ☐₄
A U.S. income tax return will not be filed.	(Skip to 62) ☐₅	A U.S. income tax return will not be filed. (Skip to 73) ☐₅

1993 total number of exemptions (Form 1040-line 6e, or 1040A-line 6e; 1040EZ filers— *see Instructions, pages 6 & 7.*)   **59.** ⊔⊔   **70.** ⊔⊔

1993 Adjusted Gross Income (AGI-Form 1040-line 31, 1040A-line 16, or 1040EZ-line 4, or *see Instructions, pages 6 & 7.*)   **60.** $_____.00 — TAX FILERS ONLY — **71.** $_____.00

1993 U.S. income tax paid (Form 1040-line 46, 1040A-line 25, or 1040EZ-line 8)   **61.** $_____.00   **72.** $_____.00

1993 Income earned from work   Student   **62.** $_____.00   Father   **73.** $_____.00

1993 Income earned from work   Spouse   **63.** $_____.00   Mother   **74.** $_____.00

1993 Untaxed income and benefits   (yearly totals only)

Social security benefits   **64.** $_____.00   **75.** $_____.00

Aid to Families with Dependent Children (AFDC or ADC)   **65.** $_____.00   **76.** $_____.00

Child support received for all children   **66.** $_____.00   **77.** $_____.00

Other untaxed income and benefits from Worksheet #2, page 11   **67.** $_____.00   **78.** $_____.00

1993 Title IV Income Exclusions from Worksheet #3, page 12   **68.** $_____.00   **79.** $_____.00

Section H: Information Release
80-91. What college(s) do you plan to attend in 1994-95?

(Note: By answering this question, you are giving permission to send your application data to the college(s) you list below.)

Housing codes	1 = on-campus 3 = with parent(s)	
	2 = off-campus 4 = with relative(s) other than parent(s)	

	College name	Address (or code, see Instructions, page 7)	City	State	Housing codes
80.					81.
82.					83.
84.					85.
86.					87.
88.					89.
90.					91.

92. Do you give the U.S. Department of Education permission to send information from this form to the financial aid agencies in your state as well as to the state agencies of all of the colleges listed above?   Yes ☐₁ No ☐₂

(States and colleges may require additional information and may have their own deadlines for applying for financial aid. Be sure to see "Deadlines for State Student Aid" in Instructions, page 10.)

93. Check this box if you give Selective Service permission to register you. *(See Instructions, page 8.)*   ☐₁

AFSA (continued)

94–95. Read and Sign

Certification: All of the information provided by me or any other person on this form and in Section I, if completed, is true and complete to the best of my knowledge. I understand that this application is being filed jointly by all signatories. If asked by an authorized official, I agree to give proof of the information that I have given on this form and in Section I, if completed. I realize that this proof may include a copy of my U.S., state, or local income tax return. I also realize that if I do not give proof when asked, the student may be denied aid.

94. Everyone giving information on this form must sign below. If you do not sign this form, it will be returned unprocessed.

1 Student _____

2 Student's Spouse _____

3 Father/Stepfather _____

4 Mother/Stepmother _____

95. Date completed ☐☐ ☐☐ Year 1994 ☐
Month   Day   1995 ☐

School Use Only
Dependency override: enter I ☐
Title IV Inst. Number ☐☐☐☐☐☐☐☐
FAA signature: 1 _____

MDE Use Only (Do not write in this box.)	Spec. handle ☐	No. copies ☐

If you (and your family) have unusual circumstances, such as:
- tuition expenses at an elementary or secondary school,
- unusual medical or dental expenses, not covered by insurance,
- a family member who is a dislocated worker, or
- other unusual circumstances that might affect your eligibility for student financial aid, you should—
  Check with the financial aid office at your college.

Preparer's Use Only
(For preparers other than student and parents. Student and parents, sign above. See Instructions, page 8.)

Preparer's name

_____
Last   First   M.I.

Firm's name and address (or preparer's, if self-employed)

_____
Firm name

_____
Number and street (Include apt. no.)

_____
City   State   ZIP code

96. Employer identification number (EIN) ☐☐☐☐☐☐☐☐☐

97. Preparer's social security number ☐☐☐☐☐☐☐☐☐

Certification:
All of the information on this form and in Section I, if completed, is true and complete to the best of my knowledge.

98. Preparer's signature   **Date**

— ATTENTION —

If you are filling out the GRAY and WHITE areas, go to Instructions, page 8, and complete WORKSHEET A. This will tell you whether you must fill out Section I. If you meet certain tax filing and income conditions, you may skip Section I.

If you are filling out the BLUE and WHITE areas, go to Instructions, page 8, and complete WORKSHEET B. This will tell you whether you must fill out Section I. If you meet certain tax filing and income conditions, you may skip Section I.

Section I: Asset Information

	STUDENT (& SPOUSE)	PARENTS
		106. Age of your older parent ☐☐
Cash, savings, and checking accounts	**99.** $_____.00	**107.** $_____.00
Other real estate and investments value (Don't include the home.)	**100.** $_____.00	**108.** $_____.00
Other real estate and investments debt (Don't include the home.)	**101.** $_____.00	**109.** $_____.00
Business value	**102.** $_____.00	**110.** $_____.00
Business debt	**103.** $_____.00	**111.** $_____.00
Farm value (See Instructions, pages 8 & 9.)	**104.** $_____.00	**112.** $_____.00
Farm debt (See Instructions, pages 8 & 9.)	**105.** $_____.00	**113.** $_____.00

MAKE SURE THAT YOU HAVE COMPLETED, DATED, AND SIGNED THE APPLICATION.
Mail the application to: Federal Student Aid Programs, P.O. Box 4054, Iowa City, IA 52243

What Happens After I Send In My Application?

Once you have completed and mailed your application(s) for financial aid, prepare to wait. It will take approximately four weeks for your forms to be processed. Depending on the forms you were required to submit, your application will either be processed by the U.S. Department of Education or a private organization such as CSS. At the end of this four-week period, you will receive a Student Aid Report (SAR) instructing you to:

- Make corrections on the forms you've submitted. The forms will then have to be resubmitted and take another two to three weeks to process.

- Confirm or provide documentation as proof of the information on your applications.

- Submit your SAR to the financial aid office at your college or university if your eligibility for aid has been determined.

QUICK TIP: *If four weeks have passed since you submitted your financial aid application and you haven't received an SAR or further instructions, you can confirm the status of your application by calling the College Scholarship Service at (301) 722-9200. You can also write to:*

Federal Student Aid Information Center
P.O. Box 84
Washington, DC 20044

Make sure to include your name (as written on the application), your address, social security number, signature, and birth date.

STUDENT AID REPORT (SAR)

The SAR is a summary of all the information contained in your financial aid application. Your estimated Family Contribution (FC) figure is determined from that information and also appears on the first page of the SAR. Based on your estimated Family Contribution, the SAR will indicate whether or not you are eligible to receive a Pell Grant. If your estimated FC is $2,100 or less, you are considered eligible to receive funds from the Pell Grant program. (To determine your approximate FC amount, see page 17).

If you are eligible to receive a Pell Grant, your SAR will be divided into three separate sections:

Part I (Summary of Information): This section summarizes all of the information that was provided on your application for financial aid. It states your estimated FC and eligibility status for other types of aid.

Part II (Correction & Review): This section is used to make changes on any false or incorrect information that appears on your SAR. Go over this part very carefully, and make sure that everything is accurate. If not, make any necessary changes in the "correct answer" area. You must then sign the statement on the bottom of Part 2 and return this page only to the address given! CSS will re-evaluate the corrections and new information, and send you a new SAR within two to three weeks.

Part III (Payment Voucher): If you are eligible for a Pell Grant, this section will be included along with Parts I and II of your SAR. This acts as a voucher for payment of your Pell Grant. All three sections must be sent to your school's financial aid office before June 30. The school then determines how much money you'll receive through the Pell Grant and other state and federal aid programs.

If you are not eligible to receive any assistance through the federal Pell Grant program, your SAR will contain Parts I and II only. Go through the exact process as described above and submit your SAR to the financial aid office at your college or university. Your school will then determine your eligibility for other forms of aid.

> **QUICK TIP:** *It is possible that your financial aid office may adjust your estimated FC or the cost of your college education, making you eligible for more aid than originally determined. College and university aid offices take into account special circumstances in which the student or family runs into some unexpected financial difficulties (such as medical bills, dislocated worker, disabilities, etc.) that affect the amount the family is able to contribute. If you feel you qualify for these unusual circumstances, contact your financial aid office immediately.*

Your SAR may be returned to you without the determination of your eligibility. This usually happens when mistakes have been made in the completion of the financial aid application(s). If this is the case, your SAR will contain Parts I and II only. Follow the review and correction instructions very carefully, then sign and return Part II to the address given. You'll receive another SAR in two to three weeks.

Students who would like their financial information sent to more than eight colleges can use the Additional College Request (ACR) form included in the SAR.

Call the Federal Student Aid Information Center/CSS at (301) 722-9200 for:

- An additional copy of your SAR.

- A status check on your application.

- Answers to any questions you may have about your SAR.

- Instructions on how to change your address. To correct your address, you must send an inquiry with your signature to the address listed on the previous page.

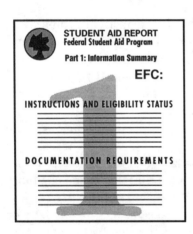
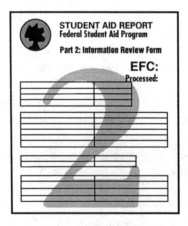

FINANCIAL AID APPLICATION PROCESS

STUDENT

❶ Student submits complete FAF / AFSA to ACT or CSS shortly after the first of the year

❺ Student sends SAR to the school by June 30

❸ Student receives Student Aid Report (SAR) from ACT or CSS

ACT / CSS

SCHOOL

❹ Family Contribution figures are sent to the school's Financial Aid Office from ACT or CCS, or the Department of Education

❻ The school determines the amount of aid the student will receive

❷ ACT or CSS sends the forms to the Department of Education, where the Family Contribution is determined

DEPARTMENT OF EDUCATION

Other Information

Student Financial Services

Common Financial Aid Questions

Q. Do I need to be accepted to a school before I apply for financial aid?

A. No, most schools do not notify students of their acceptance until after the application deadlines for financial aid. Applications for financial aid are available in November of each year, so get an application and fill it out immediately.

Q. Once I've received financial aid, do I have to reapply every year?

A. Yes.

Q. When is the deadline for financial aid?

A. Anytime before May 1.

Q. What financial contribution is a student expected to put towards his or her education?

A. Most students are required to put at least fifty percent of their prospective earnings towards to their education, and thirty to thirty-five percent of their savings, if they have any.

Q. What happens if I can't meet my expected contribution?

A. If you can't come up with the required amount, you'll most likely have to take out a loan to cover any unmet expenses.

Q. Do male students have to be registered with the Selective Service to be eligible for aid?

A. Yes. Male students 18 years or older must be registered to be considered eligible for aid.

Q. What if my parents cannot meet their contribution, or are experiencing unusual financial difficulties?

A. Usually if your parents are unable to meet their contribution, they (or you) will have to take out a loan to cover the outstanding portion. If the difficulties are a result of unusual circumstances, contact the financial aid offices at the schools to which you are applying and explain your family's situation in detail. You will be asked to provide specific financial documentation.

Q. If I only go to school part-time, can I still receive financial aid?

A. All federal programs grant assistance to students enrolled at least half-time.

Q. Will my parents' assets (home, business, or farm) be a factor in determining their expected contribution?

A. No. Home and farm values are not included in determining the projected parental contribution. Business is taken into consideration, but with special protection on this and all other assets.

Q. How many forms do I need to fill out?

A. To qualify for financial aid, you will need to either submit the FAF or AFSA, depending on your state. Some states require the completion of independent forms for state aid or scholarships. Check with all the schools to which you are applying to find out which forms you will need to submit.

Q. How much "free" financial aid will I receive?

A. This depends on your need factor. Almost every financial aid applicant will receive some free aid through the Pell Grant or SEOG program. Most students have to take out small loans to cover remaining college expenses.

Q. Are federal and state aid the only available resources for financial aid?

A. No. There are thousands of private scholarships and grants available from corporations and organizations nationwide.

Q. What happens if I don't get my financial aid application in on time?

A. Always turn in applications on time. Financial aid is awarded to eligible students who turn their applications in on time. However, if you miss a deadline, loans are available, but most likely there will be no "free" money left in the Pell Grant or SEOG programs. You will also be too late to qualify for the Perkins Loan.

Q. If I don't receive financial aid my first year in school, should I try again next year?

A. Yes. The amount and requirements for financial aid change every academic year (along with your financial situation). If you need assistance to cover tuition and expenses, apply.

Q. Once my financial aid is awarded, how will I receive it?

A. Every school has its own disbursement system, so check with the financial aid office at your college or university. Most schools disburse aid during the first week of classes.

Q. Do you have to be considered an independent to be eligible for financial aid?

A. No. Dependents and independents are both eligible to receive aid. The only difference between the two is that parents of dependent students are expected to contribute to the cost of their child's education.

Q. Should I apply for aid if I have siblings in college who are receiving aid?

A. Definitely. The more brothers and sisters you have applying for aid while attending college, the more your eligibility and the amount of aid you may receive increases.

Q. If I have a student loan, when do I have to start paying it back?

A. This depends on the type of loan you have. If you have a Stafford or Perkins Loan, repayment starts six months after you finish school. Payment with other loans usually begins immediately, but both the interest and payment on the balance can be deferred (postponed) while you're enrolled as a half-time or full-time student. However, deferment on these types of loans will increase the principal balance due to the accrued interest.

Q. How long do I have to repay my loans?

A. Most loans allow you to make monthly payments during a ten-year period.

Q. How often do the rules and regulations of financial aid change?

A. The laws are constantly changing. It's important to familiarize yourself with the new regulations every academic year.

Q. Does it cost anything to apply for financial aid?

A. Companies such as ACT and CSS charge about $9.75 and up for application processing. The exact fee is on the form and must be mailed in with the application. Federal and state applications are free.

Q. I don't know which of several schools I'm going to attend. And they all use different financial aid forms. Do I have to fill out two separate forms?

A. No. Choose the one you want to use. When you receive your Student Aid Report (SAR), approximately four weeks after submitting your application, call CSS and request a duplicate to send to the other school.

Financial Aid Terms and Definitions

Acknowledgment Report A form that summarizes the financial data from the financial aid form and shows the estimated family contribution. Parents will receive this form in order to confirm the information and make changes if necessary.

American College Testing Program (ACT) One of the two companies the government relies on to analyze family financial status and determine the expected family contribution. They send this information to colleges selected by the student. There is usually a fee for this process.

Application for Federal Student Aid (AFSA) The federal form that is used only when students want to apply for federal aid. For more information see page 159.

Assets Anything that is owned. When determining financial need assets include: cash, real estate, personal property, investments, savings accounts, etc.

Award Letter (also known as a **Financial Award Letter**) A letter that is sent to the student from the financial aid office outlining the financial aid package offered to the student. The student then needs to sign and return this letter to accept the aid that is offered.

Campus-based Program A financial aid program that is funded by state or federal money, but administered through the financial aid office of the participating school.

Cancellation (forgiveness) A deduction from the original balance a student owes on a loan. Cancellations are granted for work in a certain profession or under other specific conditions.

College Scholarship Service (CSS) One of the two services that the government and colleges rely on to determine the family's expected contribution. The major form that the CSS uses is the Financial Aid Form (FAF).

College Work Study A form of federal financial aid in which the student's wage is subsidized eighty percent by the government and twenty percent by the employer. For more information see page 26.

Conditional Scholarship A type of scholarship where specified conditions must be met, and, if they are not, the scholarship is revoked or converted into a loan.

Consolidation A payment option for students with multiple loan debts. Consolidation allows borrowers to combine the principals and pay in one monthly installment for up to twenty-five years.

Cooperative Educational Plan (CO-OP) A program that allows students to split time between work and study in order to earn money to finance their education. This can be done either through work and study during the same term or alternating one term for work and one for study. The job usually pertains to the student's major.

Cost of College An estimate of the future costs of attending a certain college for an academic period. This figure is used in determining the financial need of a student.

Default The failure to repay a student loan according to the terms that were specified in the promissory note. Upon default, the school, lender, or government agency can take legal action to ensure repayment.

Deferment A postponement of the payment of the principal and the interest on a loan to a future date. Many of the federal loan programs have some sort of deferment program.

Dependent Student A classification that says that the student is dependent on his or her parents for financial support.

Dislocated Worker A state agency must determine that a person has been unemployed for a specific amount of time, notified of termination, or previously self-employed but economic conditions resulted in job loss. If spouses or parents of aid recipients are classified as dislocated workers, the expected amount of family contribution may be less.

Family Contribution The amount calculated by using a standard need analysis formula that tells how much the family must pay towards the student's education. This number is then used to determine the student's financial need.

Financial Aid Form (FAF) The form that is used by the College Scholarship Service to gather financial information from the family in order to determine financial need.

Financial Aid Package The total aid that is given to the student, including public and private funds. This will include all scholarships, grants, loans, and work/study that are included for the student. The financial aid package is shown in detail in the award letter.

Financial Aid Transcript A record of all the federal financial aid that a student has ever received. Many schools require this form from the student when transferring to another school.

Grace Period A period of time after college graduation in which a student does not have to start repaying a loan. This usually applies to the Stafford Loan Program when the student has six to nine months before having to start repayment.

Grants A financial gift to students that does not have to be paid back. Most grants are awarded on a need basis. For more information see page 8.

Guarantee Agency The state agency that administers the Stafford, PLUS, and SLS programs in their state. This agency deals with insuring the loans and sets limitations within federal guidelines.

Half-Time A student must be attending school at least half-time in order to qualify for many types of federal aid. The criteria for half-time varies from college to college. General guidelines are as follows:

- For schools using semester, trimester, or quarter systems, a minimum of six semester or quarter hours per term.

- For schools not using academic terms to measure progress, at least twelve semester hours or eighteen quarter hours are required.

- For schools using clock hours to measure progress, a minimum of twelve hours per week.

Independent Student A student who is financially independent. In order to be classified as independent, a student must meet certain federal criteria. For more information see page 14.

Loan Money that is borrowed from the government, bank, credit union, or other lender and must be paid back. There is usually an interest charge associated with it. For more information see page 8.

Need Analysis The actual process that the CSS and the ACT use when determining the amount of financial need for each student. For more information see page 18.

Origination Fee A fee that a lender may charge in order to subsidize the cost of a low interest loan. This fee is taken out as a percentage of the loan when it is originally issued.

Parental Contribution The expected amount contributed by your parents toward your college expenses.

Parental Loans for Undergraduate Students (PLUS) Loans given to parents to help finance their children's education. For more information see page 34.

Pell Grant A strictly need-based type of financial aid. The money is given by the federal government and does not need to be paid back. For more information see page 24.

Pell Grant Index (PGI) The outcome from a series of calculations based on your federal student aid report. The index number appears on your Student Aid Report and determines the amount of Pell Grant money that should be included in your financial aid package. For more information see page 24.

Promissory Note A legal document that you must sign when you are awarded a loan. It specifies the conditions, repayment terms, and your obligation to use the money for education-related expenses only.

Reserve Officer Training Corps (R.O.T.C.) A program offered by the Air Force, Army, Marines, and Navy that provides scholarships and on-campus officer training. For more information see page 27.

Satisfactory Academic Progress A certain level of academic achievement, usually measured by grade point average, that must be achieved and maintained by the student while earning a degree. The grade point average standard is different for each school, so you must check each school to find their standard for academic progress.

- If you are enrolled in a program that is at least two years long, and the first time you received financial aid was on or after July 1, 1987, then you must maintain at least a "C" average by the end of the second year. In order to continue receiving financial aid, you must maintain this average throughout the rest of the course of study.

Scholarship A type of financial aid that you do not need to pay back. Scholarships are given for a variety of reasons, including academic excellence, talents, race, religion, group affiliations, etc. They can also be based on need. Non-need based scholarships are awarded because of achievements or talents, while need-based scholarships are awarded along with a financial aid package.

Student Aid Report (SAR) A report that is sent to you after you apply for federal financial aid. This report contains the information necessary for financial aid officers to evaluate the amount of the Pell Grant that will be included in your financial aid package. For more information see page 165.

Student's Contribution The calculated amount you should be able to provide to cover a portion of the expenses incurred while attending college. It is calculated from your expected income, assets, and benefits.

Stafford Loan Formerly the Guaranteed Student Loan. A need-based, long-term, low-interest rate loan that is subsidized by the government and awarded by an outside financial institution. For more information see page 30.

Statement of Education Purpose This is sent with the Student Aid Report (SAR) and you must sign it to assure the government that the money awarded will go exclusively to education-related expenses. The school you attend or apply to may have a similar report that you must sign.

Supplemental Education Opportunity Grants (SEOG) A campus-based grant program that usually is a supplement to Pell Grants. For more information see page 25.

Supplemental Loans for Students (SLS) Loans given to students which are not based on need. For more information see page 37.

Waiver An arrangement by the school that allows non-residents (out-of-state students and foreign students) to attend that school at the resident tuition rate.

Important Phone Numbers

The following list of important phone numbers can help you answer any questions you may have about the student aid forms or other financial aid programs.

FEDERAL AND STATE AID PHONE NUMBERS

☎ (202) 833-4000 National Education Association
- Provides sources of information on student aid

☎ (800) 826-9947 Student Loan Marketing Association (Sallie Mae)
- Provides information regarding loan repayment and consolidation

☎ (301) 722-9200 Federal Student Aid Information Center
- Reports whether application has been processed
- Sends out a duplicate copy of the SAR
  The hearing impaired can call (800) 730-8913.

☎ (800) 4FED-AID Federal Financial Aid Information Center
- Helps file a student's application or correct an SAR
- Checks on whether a school takes part in Federal State Aid Programs, or if the school has a high default rate
- Explains student eligibility requirements
- Explains the process of determining financial aid awards
- Mails information that gives and explains financial aid facts

☎ (609) 951-1025 College Scholarship Service
- Analyzes and processes the Financial Aid Form (FAF)
- Answers specific questions about filling out the FAF
- Reports on the status of the FAF Application
- Supplies additional forms upon request

☎ (319) 337-1200 America College Testing Program (ACT)
- Reports on the status of financial aid applications
- Provides test registration dates and test scores

☎ To find out more about the military's financial aid options, call this number to locate the recruiting office nearest you.

• Army	(800) USA-ARMY
• National Guard	(800) 638-7600
• Air Force	(800) 423-USAF
• Marines	(800) MAR-INES

U.S. Department of Education
400 Maryland Avenue Southwest
Washington, DC 20202
(202) 708-5366 or (800) 433-3243

REGIONAL OFFICES

REGION I: (Connecticut, Maine, Massachusetts, New Hampshire, Rhode Island, Vermont)
Office of Student Financial Assistance
United States Department of Education
J.W. McCormack Post Office and Courthouse Building
5 Post Office Square, Room 502
Boston, MA 02109
(617) 223-9338

REGION II: (New Jersey, New York, Puerto Rico, Virgin Islands, Panama Canal Zone)
Office of Student Financial Assistance
United States Department of Education
26 Federal Plaza, Room 36-118
New York, NY 10278
(212) 264-7006

REGION III: (Delaware, District of Columbia, Maryland, Pennsylvania, Virginia, West Virginia)
Office of Student Financial Assistance
United States Department of Education
3535 Market Street, Room 16200
Philadelphia, PA 19104
(215) 596-1018

REGION IV: (Alabama, Florida, Georgia, Kentucky, Mississippi, North Carolina, South Carolina, Tennessee)
Office of Student Financial Assistance
United States Department of Education
P.O. Box 1771
Atlanta, GA 30370
(404) 331-4171

REGION V: (Illinois, Indiana, Michigan, Minnesota, Ohio, Wisconsin)
Office of Student Financial Assistance
United States Department of Education
401 South State Street, Room 700D
Chicago, IL 60605
(312) 353-0375

REGION VI: (Arkansas, Louisiana, New Mexico, Oklahoma, Texas)
Office of Student Financial Assistance
United States Department of Education
1200 Main Tower Building
Room 2150
Dallas, TX 75202
(214) 767-3811

REGION VII: (Iowa, Kansas, Missouri, Nebraska)
Office of Student Financial Assistance
United States Department of Education
10220 N. Executive Hills Boulevard, 9th Floor
Kansas City, MO 64153-1367
(816) 891-8055

REGION VIII: (Colorado, Montana, North Dakota, South Dakota, Utah, Wyoming)
Office of Student Financial Assistance
United States Department of Education
1244 Speer Boulevard, Suite 310
Denver, CO 80204
(303) 844-3676

REGION IX: (Arizona, California, Hawaii, Nevada, American Samoa, Guam, Trust Territory of the Pacific Islands, Wake Island)
Office of Student Financial Assistance
United States Department of Education
IRB Region 9
50 United Nations Plaza, Room 270
San Francisco, CA 94102
(415) 556-8382

REGION X: (Alaska, Idaho, Oregon, Washington)
Office of Student Financial Assistance
United States Department of Education
915 2nd Avenue, Room 3388
Seattle, WA 98174-1099
(206) 220-7820

Financial Aid Books

If you would like to order additional copies of books from Perpetual Press, fill out the order form below. Please include $3.00 postage and handling for the first book and $1.00 for each additional copy.

Copies

_____ $19.95   The Financial Aid Book

_____ $9.95   The Government Financial Aid Book

_____ Total copies

$ _____ Total amount

$ _____ Postage and handling

$ _____ 25% discount (if completed survey is enclosed)

$ _____ Total enclosed

Send check or money order with this form to:

Perpetual Press

P.O. Box 45628

Seattle, WA 98145-0628

Name: _____

Address: _____

City: _____

State: _____ Zip: _____

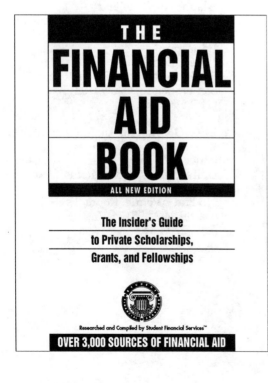

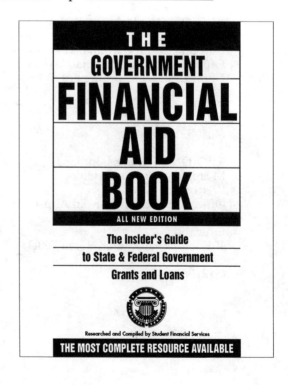

Reader Survey

Please complete this survey—detailing your financial aid experience—and receive a twenty-five percent discount off the purchase of any of Perpetual Press's Financial Aid books when bought directly through the company. See the order form on the previous page for more information.

Please answer all the appropriate questions:

1) Age: _____

2) Gender: Male   Female

3) Are you an undergraduate: Yes   No

   Year in school: _____

| Name: _____ |
| Address: _____ |
| City: _____ State: _____ |
| Zipcode: _____ |
| Phone: _____ |

4) Where did you hear about our program? _____

5) How much financial aid assistance did you receive? _____

6) How long did it take to receive your aid? _____

7) What did you do to receive your aid? _____
   _____

8) Financial Aid Search Summary: _____

State Aid

Name of award _____ Amount awarded $ _____

Action taken _____

Federal Loans

STAFFORD LOAN   Date applied _____ Amount awarded $ _____

Action taken _____

PLUS LOAN   Date applied _____ Amount awarded $ _____

Action taken _____

SLS LOAN   Date applied _____ Amount awarded $ _____

Action taken _____

PERKINS LOAN   Date applied _____ Amount awarded $ _____

Action taken _____

Federal Grants

PELL GRANT   Date applied _____   Amount awarded $ _____

Action taken _____

SEOG   Date applied _____   Amount awarded $ _____

Action taken _____

The Government Financial Aid Book Critique

Positive Aspects: _____
_____
_____
_____

Negative Aspects: _____
_____
_____
_____

What should be added or changed? _____
_____
_____
_____
_____

Other Comments: _____
_____
_____
_____
_____
_____
_____

May we contact you for additional information   Yes   No

May we quote you in future editions?   Yes   No

Send your completed survey to:

Perpetual Press
P.O. Box 45268
Seattle, WA 98145-0628

If ordering other Financial Aid books, please enclose completed survey, order form, and payment and you will receive twenty-five percent off your order.